Willful

Willful

How We Choose What We Do

Richard Robb

Yale UNIVERSITY PRESS

New Haven & London

Yale University Press books may be purchased in quantity for educational,
business, or promotional use. For information, please e-mail
sales.press@yale.edu (U.S. office) or sales@yaleup.co.uk (U.K. office).

Set in Janson type by Integrated Publishing Solutions.
Printed in the United States of America.

Library of Congress Control Number: 2019938844
ISBN 978-0-300-24643-8 (hardcover : alk. paper)

A catalogue record for this book is available from the British Library.

This paper meets the requirements of ANSI/NISO Z39.48-1992
(Permanence of Paper).

10 9 8 7 6 5 4 3 2 1

The delights of all the worlds wanted to reveal themselves to Rabbi Aaron, but he only shook his head. "Even if they are delights," he said at last, "before I enjoy them, I want to sweat for them."

—MARTIN BUBER, *Tales of the Hasidim*

Contents

Contents

Willful

PART I

Life Is a Mixed Drink

I

Venturing beyond Purposeful Choice

I'll begin with some confessions. When the facts change, I usually don't change my opinions unless I'm backed into a corner, and then I'll change them by as little as possible. I am a workaholic. I pretend that work is a pain, but I'd be lost without it. I procrastinate because boring tasks become more exciting when I'm up against a deadline. I'm careful to buy milk at the store where it's twenty cents cheaper, yet for eighteen years I have left my Columbia University retirement account in a low-yielding money market fund and missed out on a booming stock market—despite the fact that I teach economics. And I'll occasionally go out of my way to aid a casual acquaintance even when there are far more deserving people I could help. All the while, I think of myself as a rational person.

One final confession: I'm not all that embarrassed by any of this because it's the human condition. I don't believe myself to be particularly afflicted with behavioral biases, the place to turn nowadays when we're not living up to a high standard of rationality. Well, maybe I do fall into traps from time to time, like the "endowment effect" (overvaluing things I already own) or the "Lake Wobegon effect" (rating myself a better-than-average driver, for example, along with 93 percent of Americans). It's hard to be certain—after all, behavioral economics deals with blind spots. But I don't think that biases are the cause of my pigheadedness, aversion to leisure, letting problems build up even though I know by now that an ounce of prevention is worth a pound of cure, sloppiness with personal finances, random displays of altruism, or other seemingly nonrational behavior.

Instead, I think my behavior is the result of unproblematic, intrinsically human impulses. Holding beliefs that fit with each other and with our experience, that stick together over time, is part of having an identity. Robots might turn on a dime if it would help them reach their goals, but not me. Why should I revise my beliefs to gratify the desires of the new person I might become? I've also come to realize that work, like a lot of activities, is undertaken partly for reasons we can pinpoint—such as economic gain, camaraderie with colleagues, or improved status—and partly as a game. In a game, we simply play. We act on the world, and there's little more to be said.

But it doesn't feel that way. We may choose badly or make the same mistakes again and again but at some level we feel as if we are trying to get what we want. When we do act without a purpose, we invent a reason after the fact, like a sleeping person who hears a barking dog and weaves it into the narrative of her dream. Inventing reasons in this way preserves our self-image as rational.

It might sound like I'm rejecting the backbone of economic theory, *rational choice*, but to do so would be a mistake. Rational choice has illuminated huge swaths of behavior by emphasizing that we do our best to satisfy our desires with the information and resources at our disposal; we compare all available options and choose the one we prefer over the others.

I'm not launching an attack on this theory; far from it. I start out each semester defending rational choice against two objections that students usually raise: they don't feel like calculating machines and they are not materialistic. The first concern is unwarranted, because your actions may adhere to rational choice whether you know it or not. Arthur Schopenhauer tells the story of an elephant traveling through Europe, crossing many bridges. The elephant stops dead at one rickety bridge, even after seeing men and horses cross, having sensed that the bridge cannot bear its weight.[1] The defiant elephant illustrates the intuition behind much of economics: when a decision really matters, people and even animals are pretty smart.

As for the second objection, economics does not assume that people care only and unattractively about themselves and their material well-being. The satisfaction, or utility, that an individual chooses to maximize might depend on inputs like altruism, the well-being of others, or adherence to ethical standards.

Even after allowing for altruism and accepting that calculations can be intuitive, the idea of yourself as a strictly rational actor may leave you a bit queasy. Conventional thinking offers a palliative: *behavioral economics*. Behavioral economics has extended rational choice to account for biases and heuristics. A person acting with a behavioral bias also tries to satisfy her desires but routinely misses the mark. Behavioral economists hope that identifying biases will help people mend their ways and act in conformity with economic models. If rational choice theory conceives of people as robots whose behavior is determined by their preferences, then behavioral economists believe that those robots are badly programmed.

Both rational choice and behavioral economics assume that action is purposeful, that people seek the outcomes that best gratify their preexisting desires. People either know their preferences and can describe them out loud, or sense them and act as if they understood what they wanted. The purposeful choice model can explain many things, but not everything. Certain actions are undertaken not for any tangible benefit but for their own sake. They cannot be ranked against, or traded for, other actions. These actions belong to a second realm of behavior that is neither rational nor irrational, but *for-itself*.

Suppose a woman is about to jump into a river to save her drowning husband. We would not expect her to behave rationally, that is, to calculate the present value of the future benefits that she might derive from keeping her husband alive multiplied by the probability she will be able to save him (net of the probability he will save himself without her help) and then deduct the probability that she will drown multiplied by the value she attributes to her own life. It's good enough that the drowning person is her husband whom she loves. Any justification, any model or calculation, any attempt to validate her action as a realization of some general principle, would be weaker than that fact. Any additional reason for her decision would be, in the words of the philosopher Bernard Williams, "one thought too many."[2]

The distinction here is not in the magnitude of the decision. A great deal of everyday non-husband-rescuing behavior belongs to the for-itself realm. In the 1942 Preston Sturges screwball comedy *The Palm Beach Story*, an elderly Texas sausage magnate, the "Wienie King," decides to lend a hand to penniless Claudette Colbert. She reminds him of himself when he was young and poor, so in a spontaneous, one-time act of mercy, he peels off $700 from his money roll, gives it to her, and says, "so long." The Wienie King can't help everyone he meets even though other potential recipients may be more worthy of aid. His for-itself gesture to Colbert was not predictable; he just did as he liked.

While neither the husband rescuer nor the Wienie King acts on the basis of any calculation in these instances, they surely do in other contexts. I'm not asking you to jettison purposeful choice altogether, only to recognize that there's more to the story. Perhaps most of your behavior fits into the purposeful model—sometimes you're a rational agent, confident of the best course of action and able to explain your reasoning; sometimes you're a super-smart elephant who knows intuitively what action is optimal; and sometimes you're the victim of behavioral biases. But then, at other times, you're none of the above.

Admittedly, I'm an unlikely advocate for the idea that motives don't have to be purposeful and behavior doesn't have to be maximizing, that we're not always trying to pick the best available option given the information at hand. My stance is incongruous not only because I am an economist but also because I was trained at the University of Chicago, the high temple of rational choice economic theory, and still teach it enthusiastically to my students.

Drunk on Theory

I came to the realization that not all our actions have a purpose in a long and roundabout way.

I began the 1980s drunk on neoclassical economics, the theory that assumes people choose rationally and that supply and demand are in equilibrium, and then tries to explain as much of the world as it possibly can. As a PhD candidate at the University of Chicago, I saw people acting rationally everywhere I looked. Economic theory applied not just to money and markets, but to everything. Why did the A&P package fresh green beans in little cartons? Simple: if the store placed loose beans in large bins, consumers would hunt for the best ones up to the point where the extra benefit equaled their wage. The store eliminated wasteful search by selling randomly selected beans to everyone. Consumers would pay more to avoid wasting time competing for quality. Should the A&P put the best beans on top of each package where they'd be visible to consumers? No, because the store would have to pay workers to hide the lower-quality ones, and rational consumers would learn to discount appearances. My classmates and I told stories like this all day long. Gradually, we thought, the world was revealing its unseen order.

Not that doubt didn't creep in around the edges. We wondered why we'd chosen to live at a lower standard of comfort than if we had tried some pursuit other than graduate school at Chicago. We had little money. It was freezing cold. My apartment was so infested with roaches, I'd given up trying to kill them. Approximately 80 percent of the entering class would be tossed out before receiving a PhD. A few of us had been accepted to equally prestigious programs but chose to tough it out at Chicago with its notoriously difficult qualifying exams. We told ourselves that attending the University of Chicago was the best way to build human capital—capital that would lead to reasonably high earnings in stimulating academic careers. But deep down, we knew that wasn't the real reason. Somehow, we liked that it was hard. Our attraction to struggle seemed perverse as we tried to reconcile our actions with a cherished theory that felt not quite right.

Early on in graduate school, my classmates and I stumbled on behavioral economics, which was then emerging as an alternative to rational choice orthodoxy. Cognitive biases were documented in all sorts of laboratory experiments. In one famous experiment, subjects were indifferent between receiving $10 immediately and receiving $21 in one year. They were also indifferent between paying $10 immediately and paying $15 in one year. Since a rational person ought to be willing to trade off small amounts of cash now for cash in one year at a single discount rate, whether paying or receiving, this discrepancy was interpreted as evidence of "gain-loss asymmetry"—meaning that people need more compensation to delay gains than they are willing to pay to delay losses.[3]

Maybe it was that easy. If this were the case, all we had to do was document biases through experiments, like the one on gain-loss asymmetry, and adjust our models accordingly. Rational choice, with all its insights into markets and many other aspects of human behavior, could largely be preserved. But in the end, behavioral economics did not seem to be the solution to what we thought neoclassical theory was lacking. Usually, when behavioral economics offered a psychological solution for some ostensible puzzle, we could explain the data with rational choice if we worked hard enough. With the gain-loss asymmetry experiment, what about the cost of collecting the debt from the professor running the experiment? Subjects receiving a payment should be inclined to take the money now rather than have to track down the professor in a year and convince him to pay. Compensation of $11 for credit risk and inconvenience of collecting seems reasonable. Likewise, subjects who have to pay would be smart to gamble $5 in hopes that the professor would forget all about collecting and they'd never hear from him again. Considering these factors, the experimental results made sense.

Ultimately, my classmates and I likened the behavioral economists' experiments to optical illusions: entertaining and sometimes instructive, but hardly central to everyday life. In the absence of any better ideas, I made an uneasy peace with economic theory. I accepted that behavior is purposeful and choice is mostly rational with a bit of cognitive bias tossed into the mix.

After graduating in 1985, I took a job in the bond business in Chicago. As time passed, I remained convinced of the power of neoclassical economics and wary of the popular alternatives. Yet I also grew increasingly uncomfortable with the extent to which the traditional model failed to square with my own life.

First, I found plenty of truth in the saying that the journey is more important than the destination, even though the journey has little place in a worldview predicated on purposeful choice. On the job, I became blissfully lost in challenges that took on their own meaning. Sport often seemed like an apt analogy for how I competed to outsmart the markets and how my firm competed as a team against other firms.

Second, I was troubled by how I clung to my beliefs, more or less, even when they came in conflict with new data or the views of experts. I was amazed by the wide range of opinions I encountered outside the graduate school bubble. Why didn't all these supposedly rational actors converge on the common view that was best supported by the evidence?

Third, while some of my dealings with other people could be understood in terms of rational choice, as I had been taught, many could not. They were more complicated, or perhaps less complicated, than I could explain. Why, for example, would I give this person a break today but not tomorrow, and why not someone else equally close to me or equally worthy? A cost-benefit calculation didn't always apply.

Finally, I began to wonder what effect seeing the world in terms of rational choice has on our inner lives. Does removing everything from its context to determine the rate of exchange at which we would trade this for that—even if subconsciously—impoverish our experience? I wondered whether John Maynard Keynes might have been right when he warned, the "pseudo-rational view of human nature [leads] to a thinness, a superficiality, not only of judgment, but also of feeling."[4]

Theory Collides with Evidence

In 1992, I moved to New York City to become the head options trader for the derivatives subsidiary of the Dai-Ichi Kangyo Bank (DKB), Japan's largest bank at the time. I came to love DKB. My job was a sport that I could play every day. The work felt important—we were solving problems that mattered to the bank and its clients—and the challenges we faced were stimulating and continually shifting. Eventually I was promoted to global head of DKB's derivatives and securities subsidiaries in New York, London, and Hong Kong. The job left me with little leisure time, but that was okay. There was nothing I'd rather do.

My most memorable experience at DKB came during the Asian crisis in November 1998. Vaunted Japanese financial institutions like Nippon Credit, Long-Term Credit Bank of Japan, and Yamaichi Securities had gone bust, and DKB was teetering on the brink. We were set to underwrite our third Japanese auto-loan-backed security for the giant consumer finance company Orico, but the managers in Tokyo told me to cancel the deal. They were worried we would fail to sell Orico's securities to investors and embarrass the bank.

I was enraged. I had committed to raising this money for Orico and was looking forward to demonstrating that DKB could proceed with business as usual even when others had lost their nerve. I told my bosses in Tokyo that I would quit, and probably everyone else on the team would too, unless we were allowed to complete the deal. In response to this threat (a bluff), we were allowed to proceed. We agreed to cut the size of the offering and promised to sell every last bond. If we failed, we would not have the chance to quit; we would be fired. The DKB bond sales force rallied to the challenge, and the day the deal closed was one of collective joy.

Why should I have cared whether DKB canceled a deal? Why

am I still talking about it twenty years later? An economist might argue that I was concerned that a failure would cause my future earnings prospects to drop, either within the bank or if I looked for a new job. But that wasn't it. The grown-ups were going to take away our ball in the middle of the game. It was no more than that.

It was getting harder and harder for me to cling to the view of work as a sacrifice of leisure to get money for consumption. I could not have bought my experiences at DKB—they were not for sale, and even if they were, it would have made no sense to pay for them. Nor could I determine a price at which I'd be indifferent to trading them for other things. It gnawed at me that I could not squeeze the attributes of my job into the framework of rational choice. Another sort of analysis was needed.

The game truly did end in 2000 when DKB merged with Fuji Bank and Industrial Bank of Japan. There was no role in the new bank for me. My boss told me, in a masterpiece of Japanese tact, "Frankly speaking, you are free to work anywhere you like." I gestured to our trading room. He looked down and mumbled, "Anywhere but here." I decided to enjoy some leisure time, which after ten years with the bank, I could afford. But it was not at all what I expected.

Each morning in my early retirement, I read the *New York Times*, helped make breakfast for my nine-year-old daughter and fourteen-year-old son, sent them off to school, and jogged around the reservoir in Central Park. At that point, it was 9:00 a.m. I discovered that the day is long. Weekends blended in with week-days. Sure, I was free from the annoyances that had cropped up at my job, but I didn't like it at all.

My dissatisfaction didn't arise from low income, as rational choice theory would suggest. My time at DKB had left me with ample savings, and I spent a few hours each week trading for myself. (More on that later.) Shuffling around the apartment in my slippers was a comfortable way to make enough money to cover my family's expenses.

I puzzled over this uneasiness until, one day during my abundant leisure time, I took my daughter to the Bronx Zoo. We watched the zookeeper feed the tigers a lunch of fish encased in blocks of ice. The tigers had to strip away the ice before they could eat; they seemed to relish the struggle. Suddenly, it became clear: I was like the tiger, except the zookeeper was feeding me all the ice-free fish I wanted, whenever I wanted. I knew my situation was fortunate and, to many, enviable, yet I craved a challenge. Eventually, I found two.

First, I started a hedge fund with partners in New York and London. Our fund aimed to raise money to invest in European structured credit—debt securities that package the risk of loans to individuals or companies. I could try to rationalize this undertaking in terms of wealth maximization, but in reality, starting a business put my nest egg in jeopardy. A nail-biting adventure was the way to conquer the doldrums.

I had invested in two entrepreneurial ventures before this

fund, and both were disasters. They dragged on and on, sucking up more money than anyone had intended because we always believed that a change in our fortunes was just around the corner. I hoped that things would be different this time, even though the past is supposed to be the best predictor of the future and all that.

Our fund got off to a rocky start. Although we were able to swiftly raise $11 million, that's not enough for a viable hedge fund. We met with around a hundred potential investors and kept hearing the same message: "You'll be a safer investment at $50 million than at $11 million. You'll be more diversified and have better access to financing. Come back when you're bigger." We needed to reach a critical mass quickly. If no one invested, no one else would invest. If many invested, many more would join in. We were stuck in the bad equilibrium. Because we had chosen to register with the Securities and Exchange Commission, the law required us to raise $25 million in the first ninety days. We fell short of the mark and faced the embarrassing prospect of having to deregister. Our original investors began to make noises about getting their money back.

All at once, our luck turned. The SEC inexplicably gave us a one-month extension, and then a new investor swooped in with $40 million. Other investors fell into place, and within five years we had $2 billion.

My miserable spell of unemployment and sense of rejuvenation prompted by starting the fund led me right back to the same old dilemma. I could no longer accept the traditional economic model that saw a trade-off between work and leisure and emphasized the importance of consumption. Yet I wasn't ready to turn my back on the orthodoxy altogether. In a way, my experience trading bonds in Chicago, working at DKB, and starting a hedge fund actually reinforced my faith in rational choice theory. Practically every day, useful insight came from assuming that people optimized and markets were in equilibrium. Economic theory often felt like my secret weapon.

The second challenge I took on was teaching microeconomics at Columbia's School of International and Public Affairs, first as an adjunct and then in a full-time position. In 2002, a year after I started teaching, I had the great fortune of meeting Edmund Phelps. With his project at Columbia's Center on Capitalism and Society, he intended to reformulate economics for the modern world. The center sought a theory to describe "real human beings who are not only acquisitive and risk averse but also inquisitive and adventurous and who sometimes feel the need to take a plunge, to leap into the unknown." This was new. I especially liked the phrase "not only." There had to be room for both.

The realization that a second realm sits alongside purposeful choice was the turning point for me. Why should one grand system explain it all? People not only seek to gratify desires, but also choose obstacles to overcome. If they succeed, or tire of their project and abandon it, new challenges will arise. It's natural that this is hard to see, since action can feel more intentional than it really is. We often act first, then invent a cause for that action, which we usually describe in terms of seeking pleasure or avoiding pain.[5]

"This Tricky Profit"

Of course, I didn't discover this realm. Fyodor Dostoevsky describes acts that cannot fit into lists of preferences (in economic lingo, inputs into utility functions). He asks: "how does it happen that all these statisticians, sages, and lovers of mankind, in calculating human profits, constantly omit one profit? . . . It's no great trouble just to take it, this profit, and include it in the list. But that's the whole bane of it, that this tricky profit doesn't fall into any classification, doesn't fit into any list."[6]

This "tricky profit" that eludes all systems and models is the exercise of will. Dostoevsky continues, "Man, whoever he might be, has always and everywhere liked to act as he wants, and not at all as reason and profit dictate; and one can want even against one's own profit, and one sometimes even *positively must*. . . . [A]ll this is that same most profitable profit, the omitted one, which does not fit into any classification, and because of which all systems and theories are constantly blown to the devil."[7]

Dostoevsky's "most profitable profit" cannot fit into a list alongside all other desires in the rational choice framework. In that model, an individual is controlled by her preferences. If the exercise of will were one of those preferences, then the resulting actions would be predictable and automatic, and therefore no longer "willed." So acts that result from the exercise of will rather than the pursuit of preferences must belong to a different realm: what I call "for-itself."

Each for-itself action stands for itself without regard to whether it is better than some alternative. It is undertaken "just because." It can be a flow or a process, a self-justifying game, or a struggle to overcome a challenge that is not important in any objective way. For-itself behavior includes acting confidently based on beliefs we hold and that matter to us (whether or not those beliefs are accurate) because that's who we are. Our beliefs constitute our identity and so are not up for sale; "I yam what's I yam," declares Popeye the Sailor Man in a kind of for-itself anthem. The apparent opposite of entrenching ourselves in our beliefs— an impromptu leap out of character— is for-itself, too.

Above all, the for-itself realm emphasizes agency—an individual acting on the world. It considers time as a flow rather than as a single moment, which is all purposeful choice can truly accommodate. The purposeful model cannot explain (or be adjusted to explain) how we decide to consume now or later, to retire or continue working. Nor can it explain why we procrastinate, are inattentive to personal finances, start quixotic businesses, and persevere with projects for long stretches without evaluating whether to quit. In contrast, the more fluid for-itself model captures behavior as it unfolds over time in response to the challenges we encounter. This behavior includes spontaneous altruistic acts that no one could have predicted and heroism of the one-thought-too-many variety (e.g., the woman rescuing her husband) that transcends any rational calculus.

Just as rational choice, and perhaps behavioral economics, has shed light on the sphere of purposeful choice, a methodical approach can be developed to analyze for-itself action, although not with the same degree of rigor. My intent is to understand real-world phenomena that matter to individuals and firms and impact public policy. My method involves drawing the boundary between these two modes of action—the purposeful and the for-itself—and then explaining for-itself conduct with as much precision as I can. Most of my examples are drawn from business and investing because that's my area of expertise, but a similar analysis might be fruitful in fields like politics, education, and history.

Although my thinking has evolved out of personal experience, I believe my thesis is nearly universal. For most of us, who try to see our behavior as rational, embracing one realm to the exclusion of the other leaves us with a picture of the world that is incomplete. We strain to fit for-itself conduct into a realm where it doesn't belong and, despite all the ingenuity we may deploy, end up with unsatisfying results. Of course, I recognize that some people, when choosing how to live their lives, discount purposeful action and instead cultivate spontaneity. These people will be unmoved by my claim that there's more to life than rational choice. But these happy few may have an opposite quandary: how to reconcile the rational side of their actions with their natural grace. They, too, may wish to explore the boundary between the for-itself—their home base—and the purposeful.

On the one hand, I don't want to claim too much for my thesis. My approach will not lead to a completely unified theory of human action because such a theory is impossible. Nor do I want to deny the supremacy of the purposeful approach to behavior. While my early exhilaration with rational choice economics has faded, my conviction in its power remains. On the other hand, I am equally convinced that the purposeful choice model has serious limitations. Only by venturing beyond purposeful choice— with or without behavioral biases—can we improve our theories of many practical matters. Important aspects of our behavior (even in financial markets) are best understood not by neoclassical economics or mathematics or adding to the catalog of behavioral biases, but by reassessing basic motives, along with assumptions about how those motives relate to action. Some of our actions arise from for-itself impulses rather than the purposeful intent to satisfy desires. Recognizing the twofold nature of our behav ior will generate a truer understanding of ourselves—one that is more at ease with our experience. As Nietzsche observed: "Honey, says Heraclitus, is at the same time bitter and sweet; the world itself is a mixed drink which must constantly be stirred."[8]

2

Two Realms of Human Behavior

Before diving into the details, let's take a closer look at the categories of purposeful and for-itself behavior, define our terms, and introduce the key themes that will emerge in our investigation of this second realm.

The diagram summarizes my schema for human action.

Purposeful Choice

While much of this book will focus on the bottom fork of the diagram, for-itself action, we'll start with a quick tour of the top fork: purposeful choice. But first, let's clarify some terms. I'll use "purposeful" as an umbrella term when contrasted to "for-itself" or when I want to allow for the possibility of behavioral bias. I'll use "rational choice" to refer to economists' traditional neoclassical models or to emphasize that I'm considering choice

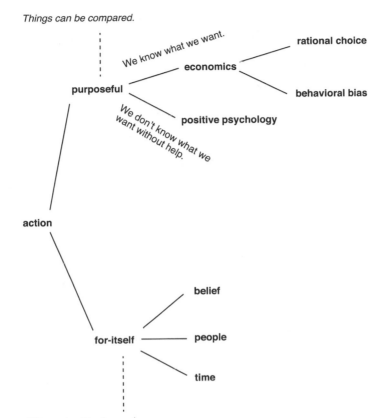

Things can be compared.

We know what we want.

economics

rational choice

purposeful

behavioral bias

We don't know what we want without help.

positive psychology

action

belief

for-itself ———— people

time

Things stand for themselves.

that is free of behavioral bias. "Cognitive bias" and "behavioral bias" will be treated as synonyms. "Preferences" will refer to desires in the purposeful realm—we know whether we would prefer to satisfy one desire over another and can rank them. The terms "wants," "needs," and "desires" will emphasize purposefulness. But, at some high level of abstraction, for-itself conduct also concerns desire and its synonyms: someone who doesn't desire an action wouldn't undertake it. The key difference is that purposeful choice deals with desires that can be compared to and traded for each other.

When we understand and evaluate the strength of our desires, we enter the purposeful sphere. Purposeful choice assumes people mostly know what they want, and when they talk about desires that they don't intend to act on, they are merely confused. As the old joke goes, two economists are walking down the street. The first one says, "I'd like to buy a car like that." The second one answers, "No, you wouldn't." That's the whole joke. The first economist doesn't want the car enough to make the required sacrifices or else he would already have bought it. He reveals his true preferences through his conduct.

Behavioral economics assumes that people understand their preferences, but that defects in their mental apparatus impair decision-making. At least one hundred and fifty behavioral biases have been identified, mostly through laboratory experiments, from the "ambiguity effect" (ruling out options when we can't assign probabilities to possible outcomes) to the "zero risk bias" (spending unwarranted amounts to reduce small risks to zero while ignoring bigger ones). Presumably, once people are made aware of their biases, they will try to correct them, choose more wisely, and become better off. Until then, the field seeks to build more accurate models of behavior.

Both rational choice and behavioral economics are effective in explaining our actions to the extent that we are indeed seeking to gratify our desires and can foresee what the consequences of our actions will be. This does not mean that we can predict what will happen with absolute certainty, but that we at least know enough about the structure of the world to assess the possible outcomes and the probability that each will occur. In practice, we're often only vaguely aware of what might happen. Rather than facing crisp, easily modeled decisions—if we take action x, then y will happen with probability p and so forth—we may feel awash in a sea of ambiguity. This reality doesn't imply that we need to toss out the apparatus of purposeful choice altogether, but does suggest that under such conditions, economists should be modest in their claims. In purposeful choice, people do their best with the information they have and spend resources to gather more information when that's the optimal course.

Nor does purposeful choice require that we have perfect knowledge of ourselves. We might get exactly what we want and then feel disappointed. We can learn through experience and, in recent decades, through positive psychology. Also called happiness research, this second branch of purposeful choice can be regarded as an aid to learning about our nature and preferences, helping us make more satisfying decisions.

Assuming that at least some people know whether or not they are happy, discovery of the cause of that happiness should be an empirical task: ask a lot of people how happy they are, find out about their lives, and analyze the data. Do happy people have high incomes? High income relative to others around them? Rising income? Or does happiness correlate with some other factor? If people are similar, we can learn about ourselves via the systematic study of others. Here, self-realization becomes a group project: having conducted surveys or brain studies and assumed people are homogeneous, positive psychologists advise us to spend more time with friends, find shorter commutes to work, and worry less about making money after reaching the upper middle class. Done in this way, happiness research effectively generates a collection of self-help tips. It may also be used as a guide for public policy—if we can objectively measure happiness, then governments can try to promote it.

Whether or not we have an accurate understanding of our desires, the steps for applying purposeful choice are the same: determine, as best we can, what those desires are; rank them, consciously or unconsciously; and choose how to satisfy them, given our resources.

For-Itself

Let's now turn to the south fork of the diagram: for-itself.

The first branch, *beliefs*, explores how we come to our beliefs and how they shape our actions. Much of the time, we stick with our beliefs regardless of the evidence. Does this make us irrationally stubborn? I don't think so. We hold onto our beliefs because they're part of our identity. Stick-to-it-ness belongs to the for-itself realm, as does an occasional leap out of character.

This is neither rational nor irrational; it's just the sort of creature we are.

A for-itself commitment to our beliefs can explain rigidities in companies and markets and why we sometimes fail to make profitable investments. An entrepreneur, for instance, may be lit up with conviction for her project, and who knows? She may turn out to be right. But the venture capitalist whom the entrepreneur approaches simply can't share her enthusiasm. The venture capitalist may be fully incentivized to unearth promising startups; she may think clearly and be open-minded, courageous, honest, and intelligent. Yet she rejects the pitch. Nothing the entrepreneur says can bridge the gap in their beliefs.

That's because the entrepreneur has been galvanized by a one-time opportunity. Its essential appeal is unique so it can't be compared to opportunities that have come before, at least as far as the entrepreneur is concerned. It stands for itself. This murky realm is where the money is made, so limits to the transmission of belief is a key neglected topic in finance.

The for-itself dimension of belief also explains why people go to so much trouble to form their own opinions. Why not simply adopt the views of an expert? The expert might be incompetent, but at least she's gone through a vetting process and, odds are, knows more than you. Still, we resist experts who tell us what we're supposed to believe. Defying them is a for-itself act of will. When expert opinion conflicts with our core beliefs, the for-itself response is to discredit the expert, shop for maverick experts, and either hang on to preexisting beliefs for as long as possible or adjust them as little as possible.

The middle for-itself branch, *people*, analyzes social relations. Without a doubt, many of our social dealings belong to the realm of purposeful choice. Performing favors in anticipation of receiving reciprocal favors down the road can help us get ahead. Or we may care so deeply about other people that their well-being enters into our own preferences and becomes part of what we maximize. Most Sundays before my wife wakes up, I go to a bakery around the corner to buy her a blueberry scone. She values the scone. I don't mind a short errand that gets me out of the house and I care about her well-being, so buying the scone optimally improves my well-being. If it's cold or rainy or I'm particularly busy, the cost to me of buying the scone is greater than the benefit, so I rationally skip it.

Yet there are situations that draw us into the unpredictable realm of spur-of-the-moment good deeds. I often see riders on the subway train hold the doors so strangers can scramble on. Not only does this break the Metropolitan Transportation Authority's rules, it strikes me as antisocial. The calculus just doesn't add up: holding the door saves one stranger the five-minute wait for the next train, but delays three hundred other passengers by ten seconds, increasing the total waiting time by forty-five minutes. If the door holder's aim is to benefit humankind, he should let the doors close.

That's what I'd always think during my ten seconds of extra waiting. For years, I considered this behavior irrational. Perhaps the door holder wanted to maximize social welfare but suffered from a cognitive bias that attributed too much importance to salient information that had captured his attention—the one stranger about to miss the train. Or perhaps he was too confused by the calculations to reason properly. But maybe the confusion was mine—I was trying to fit a for-itself act into the purposeful model. My preference for letting the doors close is the result of a calculation, while holding them open is an act of mercy that transcends calculations.

But even with this more nuanced understanding, I still let the doors slam shut. I adhere to an ethical principle—promotion of the common good—unless I have a personal connection to whomever is about to miss the train. If the cost and benefit were approximately equal, I'd be inclined to favor the single person over the abstract calculation, but a forty-five-minute social cost for one person's five-minute benefit is just too lopsided. Still, I can't really object to the door holder's defense: in a wholly spontaneous gesture, he reacted to a need as it arose.

The way we act on the world as we move through it will be treated more broadly with the final branch, *time*. Often activity that unspools over time is best understood in terms of flow, as a for-itself process of continuous choosing.

In order to explain our actions, we infer a beginning, an end, and a causal link between them. This abstraction makes it easy to freeze each moment in conscious thought, but is it an accurate characterization of life? Kierkegaard observes that we cannot continually keep ourselves "on the spear tip of the moment." Rather, he asks us to "imagine a captain of a ship the moment a shift of direction must be made; then he may be able to say: I can do either this or that. But if he is not a mediocre captain he will also be aware that during all this the ship is ploughing ahead with its ordinary velocity."[1] Simply put, time never stops so that we may evaluate alternative bundles, pick what's best, and then experience the consequences once time restarts. Purposeful choice requires that we ignore the flux and interpret action in terms of static categories. The for-itself perspective will provide us with an alternative picture of time and the way action unfolds.

From the for-itself perspective, rather than maximizing some measure of present and future well-being, we choose the obstacles that we then struggle to overcome. The chase takes on a life of its own. The importance of the chase explains the impulse to become a professional basketball player or a rock star and to persevere even as evidence mounts that the chance of success is approaching zero. Likewise, a student might complete a degree even after deciding to quit the field; she wants to finish what she started. (A rational choice economist could argue that finishing the degree raises her income because it signals grit. But the benefit of that signal is unlikely to outweigh the cost of a year of her life plus tuition.) These projects make sense only if we accept that an activity can matter beyond its ostensible purpose. A quest is about fighting over time and, when necessary, against the odds.

These battles don't have to be major undertakings. They can instead be relatively minor, or even pointless. A cook prepares a meal according to a difficult recipe even though the subtleties are likely to go unnoticed, and a tenured professor diligently improves a class after it's oversubscribed. Some of my students pull all-nighters before exams in hopes of improving their grade from an A– to an A. Even after they've secured the job they want and the baseline GPA to graduate, these students lose none of their zeal for obtaining the highest grade. They are like athletes, and this is their sport. Wearing themselves out studying, the students feel that the challenge of the exam and celebration of a victory if they win are all part of their process.

In the case of important challenges, success is often followed by a different kind of test—finding a new, equally meaningful quest. For example, what to do after you have enough money and your one and only skill is making more? Perhaps you turn to conspicuous consumption and start accumulating the status symbols that you mocked not long ago. This new pursuit might feel a bit hollow—after all, you chose it because you didn't know what else to do. Then you'll have to try something that feels more natural to you: maybe philanthropy or resetting your sights on overtaking your enemies who are more successful still.

The Significance of Authenticity

In the morning, I generally desire a cup of coffee. The quality can differ in all sorts of ways, satisfying my desires to a greater or lesser degree. I could assign a price to the small differences if I thought about it. But there is no sense in which I desire *this particular cup* of coffee; I just care about how hot it is, what it tastes like, what it costs, and so on. All potential cups are substitutes for other cups.

In purposeful choice, our aims are commensurable—one can be traded for another at some rate of exchange. This is not the case when acting for-itself. I might take on this challenge or commit to that eccentric belief for reasons I can't fully explain. I'm not optimizing when I spend ninety minutes on a Sunday emailing with a student to clear up a misunderstanding on a minor point in the lecture notes—I have many students and they have many misunderstandings. I'm not going to pretend that I break my back attending to all of them. I could spend that time more profitably and help more students by organizing a group review session. Why bother with this one?

While I can't give a precise answer, it matters that this exchange arises naturally: a current student is genuinely grappling with this week's material. It feels like he wants to understand, not to cozy up to me for a letter of recommendation or a better grade. Before the email arrived, I did not think to myself, "I hope a student emails me seeking assistance." But when it does arrive, there's a chance I'll take the bait.

A for-itself challenge can be relatively trivial or objectively important. No matter the magnitude of the challenge, it must come about organically to be experienced as authentic. A government program that paid people to dig holes and then fill them up again would be unpopular not only with taxpayers but also with diggers, since they'd know it was contrived to keep them busy.

Context is critical to for-itself action because this realm deals with unique events. This is the polar opposite of purposeful choice, which values options according to their various attributes and how well those attributes satisfy a person's fixed desires. In fact, economist Gary Becker counted stable preferences among the three key axioms of neoclassical economics (along with optimizing behavior and markets in equilibrium).[2] If our tastes bounced around randomly, rational choice theory would lack its predictive power. Of course, we may prefer a cold drink in the summer and a hot one in the winter. We may prefer variety; after an orange is chosen over an apple five times, oranges yield diminishing marginal utility and we switch to apples. Viewed at a sufficiently general level, these choices reflect coherent, stable preferences.

An ostensible paradox formulated by behavioral economist Richard Thaler has a simple resolution if we consider the importance of authenticity. Thaler points out the inconsistency of a man refusing to hire somebody to mow his lawn for eight dollars but then turning down the opportunity to mow a neighbor's similarly sized lawn for twenty dollars. Thaler attributes this paradox to cognitive bias.[3] Rational choice economists might point to different reasons for this behavior: if the man hired himself out as a mower, he could suffer diminished status among his neighbors or incur transaction costs in negotiating the terms of the job, as well as additional income tax. If he hired a mower, coordinating and monitoring would impose additional costs. But this is unconvincing: people would mow their own grass but not their neighbor's for pay, even if they could work in disguise to uphold their status, income taxes were eliminated, and quality was easy to monitor.

This paradox arises in a strict purposeful choice framework, with agents evaluating work according to factors like pay and pleasantness of the task, while ignoring authenticity. For-itself theory provides a simple explanation: some people enjoy the physical challenge of yard work. Every day the grass grows and the homeowner likes keeping it under control. Hiring oneself out as a paid laborer does not arise naturally in this context, and no practical amount of money could convert it into a challenge worth overcoming. If a behavioral economist were to explain to the person who mowed his own lawn but not his neighbor's for pay that he has been duped by cognitive bias, it's unlikely he would set up shop as a gardener. He doesn't experience this behavior as problematic, and neither should we.

The Lottery Winner's Curse illustrates the meaning we derive from engaging in authentic challenges and how lost we feel when they disappear. Imagine you are a thirty-five-year-old vice president for a big bank working in New York City. Your compensation is $200,000 annually—around four times New York City's median household income—but after taxes you have just enough to pay basic living expenses and rent the two-bedroom apartment where you live with your stay-at-home spouse and two children. Altogether, it's a fulfilling life. Your job involves the usual worries, which occupy much of your attention. You come home from work tired but satisfied that you're putting bread on the table. You have a plan to claw your way to the top and look forward to the luxuries and comforts that your family will someday be able to afford.

Your lucky day comes sooner than you expected. From out of the blue, a long-lost relative dies and leaves you a fortune, say $10 million tax free. Now what? Your job at the bank, which now adds only a pittance to your material circumstances, will start to feel pointless, yet you don't have quite enough money (or the inclination) to devote yourself to philanthropy full time.

If you complained about your dilemma, you'd find no sympathy. You're rich! And rational choice theory would offer no support: you have all the same options as before, plus the new ones that your wealth opens up. According to for-itself theory, however, maybe your good fortune wasn't so good after all, since it sabotaged your engagement with authentic challenges. You can't go back to your old life, not really, and the difficulties of striving to get ahead have been hollowed out. So far, no new challenge has presented itself in place of the old one. Deep down, you may even regret the windfall, but sadly, there's nothing to be done about it.

If a demon suddenly appeared, offering a winning lottery ticket, I imagine nearly everyone would take it. I would. But a windfall might make you miserable, as it did our banker, and, evidently, many real-life lottery winners. That result doesn't fit with purposeful choice; it belongs to the realm of for-itself.

In purposeful behavior, we optimally satisfy our preferences within the constraints of our limited resources. If those constraints are relaxed (typically through more money), we'll do better. But this is not so in the for-itself realm. This distinction will become clearer as we encounter other thought experiments throughout this book. Powerful intervening figures like the demon with the winning lottery ticket will yank individuals from their lives with offers of free gifts, control over the future, or favorable trades. But the deals will backfire, exposing the importance of context and the limits of purposeful choice.

Authenticity may not play such a crucial role in the purposeful choice model, but it's intrinsic to our engagement with everyday life. Adventures, like the time the car got a flat tire and we had to walk five miles to a gas station at night, may offer meaning richer than the satisfaction we could derive from consumption, but we do not choose such experiences—the experience chooses us. If we were to slash the tire intentionally, the resulting experience would feel like an exercise in cynicism. Still there's no reason to characterize this adventure as for-itself: once the car breaks down, rational choice ought to kick in.

Neither Realm Can Eclipse the Other

Suppose you're setting out to rent an apartment. You'll consider the features of each available option, how much you value those features, and whether they justify the price. If your income goes up, other things being equal, you'll rent a bigger and better place. Maybe you are seduced by a cunning broker or by marketing gimmicks that exploit your behavioral biases and so you choose one that's too expensive. Whether you choose well or poorly, it's purposeful: you seek to satisfy your desires for convenient location, ample size, aesthetic charm, length of lease, quality of construction, and a dozen other factors, while keeping in mind the alternative uses of the money you might save by renting someplace cheaper.

If we tried to analyze this decision through any lens other than rational choice (or purposeful choice, if biases are in play), we would miss out on all its many insights. No reasonable person chooses an apartment purely on impulse, as a one-time plunge into the chaotic unknown. If you behaved that way, you'd be in big trouble. Consciously or unconsciously, we weigh the consequences of various alternatives and pick the one that seems best, knowing what we know. Rational choice makes this comparison possible by converting disparate options into a common currency.

This mechanism goes beyond ranking and aggregating easy

comparisons. Suppose I'm considering three apartments, one downtown (D), one in midtown (M), and one uptown (U), and assume that my wife has delegated the decision to me. Midtown would provide the easiest commute because I could walk to my office and take a relatively short subway ride uptown on the one or two days each week I go to Columbia. My commute from uptown would be second best since I could walk to Columbia and ride the subway to my midtown office. Living downtown, I would have to take a medium subway ride to reach the office and a long one to reach Columbia. Comparing the commutes one at a time, I can arrive at a ranking:

Commute: M > U > D.

The largest of the three apartments is uptown, the second largest is downtown, and the smallest is in midtown.

Size: U > D > M.

My wife, Ianthe, prefers downtown to midtown and midtown to uptown. As discussed later, in Part 3, care altruism makes my utility a function of hers, so her preferences matter to me.

Ianthe: D > M > U.

There are many other factors to evaluate in choosing an apartment, but to simplify the decision, consider just these three. I might envision the internal debate as three homunculi residing in my mind, each advocating for a preference. Homunculus 1 focuses on the commute, homunculus 2 on apartment size, and homunculus 3 on pleasing my wife. Suppose the homunculi cast one vote each. In elections considering two apartments at a time, M would beat U, since homunculi 1 and 3 would vote for M, while U would beat D, since homunculi 1 and 2 would vote for U. Yet D would beat M, since D would get the votes of homunculi 2 and 3.

Election: M > U > D > M.

The homunculi would arrive at a stalemate, leaving my wife and me without a place to live.[4] I would go round and round until I fired the homunculi and switched to a different approach. I could simplify the decision by choosing to act on a single reason, focusing on the feature that is most important. For me, that's the commute, and the shortest commute is from midtown. But this simple-minded approach, which throws out troves of valuable information, is no formula for getting ahead. The smarter tack would be to quantify each variable so I can weigh factors such as "how much better is the commute from midtown than the one from downtown?" and "how much do I care about the commute versus pleasing my wife?"

Because these disparate factors become comparable with a common currency, purposeful choice can handle this decision. I might wish the decision were less complicated, but I've got to think it through.

Not all decisions are driven by such clarity of purpose. Consider the following thought experiment: after watching a documentary on TV, I decide to donate to a charity devoted to refugees. On my way to the post office to mail a $100 check, a gust of wind catches a $100 bill that happened to be tucked into my shirt pocket and blows it away. At just that moment, I receive an email from a friend who saw the same TV show and was stirred to send $100 to the same charity.

If I'm motivated solely by concern for the refugees' welfare, I should now tear up the check I was about to mail. I wanted a world in which I had $100 less and the charity had $100 more. That world is now a reality by virtue of the lost $100 bill and my friend's generosity. If I still send a $100 check, then either I truly preferred a $200 donation in the first place or the act of donation is about more than the money. Sending the check is a one-time, unique gesture. I don't donate up to the "optimal point" where the marginal benefit of the last dollar to the refugees equals its next best use in my life. Nor do I investigate every other charity to ensure that this one is the most worthy. This act of giving stands for itself.

Commingling of the Two Realms

The purposeful and for-itself are often bound together in the same activity. Work is perhaps the ultimate example of an activity that is at once purposeful and a high-stakes for-itself game. Many aspects of the labor market that are inadequately accounted for by purposeful choice can be explained neatly once we recognize that money is in part a by-product of work, rather than its exclusive driver. As Alfred Marshall wrote in *Principles of Economics*, "Just as a race-horse or an athlete strains every nerve to get in advance of his competitors, and delights in the strain; so a manufacturer or a trader is often stimulated much more by the hope of victory over his rivals than by the desire to add something to his fortune. The action of such motives as these must be studied carefully by economists; and the allowance required to be made for them will in some cases be so great as to alter perceptibly the general character of their reasonings."

The thrill of winning, "delight in the strain," and engagement with colleagues in a team sport are intangibles generated by work that many people cannot access in any other way. These intangibles help explain why some work long hours and retire late in life or even deliberately work until the day they die. They account for a housecleaner who hires cleaners for his own house and a cobbler whose children have no shoes. Both are so caught up in their jobs that they neglect duties at home. This kind of work effort is inconsistent with the rational choice trade-off between labor and leisure, but consistent with the for-itself theory of overcoming obstacles.

Many members of the middle and upper class would end up with more money if they devoted one hour less a week to work and one hour more to optimizing investments, organizing tax records, and reducing interest and fees paid to banks or credit card issuers. By focusing on personal finances, a homeowner might, for example, realize that redeeming shares in mutual funds that invest in mortgage-backed securities and using the proceeds to repay her own mortgage would cut several layers of fees. But she doesn't need to be told any of this: if all she cared about was maximizing steady-state consumption, she would have done so already.

The commingling of purposeful and for-itself also explains the phenomenon that economist Herbert Simon called "satisficing." "Satisficing" describes decision-making that falls short of optimization. A satisficing person evaluates courses of action only until she arrives at one that is "good enough." In Simon's theory, the satisficer doesn't try for the optimum because the calculations are too hard.[5]

A rational person with all the brainpower she needed, however, might want a reasonably good outcome in terms of satisfying preexisting desires while leaving room for choice. In this case, she would serve up a few acceptable options and pick one as if at random. The one she picked would come as a surprise, both to herself and to an observer. Although this might look like an irrational failure to optimize, it can be a deliberate attempt to preserve her ability to exercise her will. Satisficing thus enables us to go through our day, choosing (somewhat) freely while still doing pretty well in terms of satisfying our preferences. The two explanations for not-quite-optimizing—that is, cognitive failures and for-itself acts of will—can be distinguished empirically: un-

like satisficing, for-itself choosing applies to complicated decisions as well as simple ones that require little effort or attention.

Defaulting to Purposeful Choice

Purposeful choice is easy to understand, think about, and explain.
We are so steeped in this way of thinking that we take the question "why did you do this?" to mean "why is this optimal?" When
the true nature of our behavior is obscure, we'll default to an
explanation that lets us maintain a rational self-image.

Self-image matters to us. In *Thus Spoke Zarathustra*, Nietzsche
describes a bloodthirsty murderer who, ashamed, robs his victim
to provide a motive retroactively.[6] Having established one, he
can see himself as a rational actor rather than an incomprehen-
sible monster. Though we may have little else in common with
such a criminal, every one of us fabricates explanations for our
behavior at least some of the time. We pride ourselves in our rationality, and when prompted to explain our own actions, may
feel sheepish answering "just because." As natural storytellers, we
invent motives after the fact to explain actions that were without
clear purpose, whether to some external audience or simply for
our own benefit. Conditioned as we are to thinking in terms of
causal relationships, we reflexively assume that our choices are
motivated by a reason and buy into our own justifications.

On rare and spooky occasions, we catch ourselves splicing an
event into our memory before it could have occurred. But while
we only infrequently feel a sense of déjà vu, rationalizing a mo-

tive after we take action and experience the resulting pleasure or pain is woven into our experience.

This compulsion to identify rational motives for our actions can make it difficult to accept that some actions are simply play. Someone who earns more than she can consume in the short term is rational if she enjoys the work or wants to save for the future. Behavioral scientists examined what would happen in the absence of both conditions with an experiment in which the work was designed to be unpleasant and the subjects couldn't save. During the first five minutes, subjects could choose to listen to obnoxious white noise or to music. They earned small chocolate bars in proportion to the amount of time they listened to the obnoxious noise. They then had five minutes to consume their earnings, after which they forfeited any chocolate they did not eat. Although they had been warned of this rule in advance, subjects earned significantly more chocolate than they consumed. Additionally, subjects who earned higher wages, that is, more chocolates per unit of noise, worked about as long as subjects who received a lower wage.[7]

The researchers decided that these results pointed to a pathological tendency to "overearn," comparable to overeating. A Harvard Business School professor told the *New York Times* that the study's implications were "enormous."[8] But were they really? Instead of suffering from a newly diagnosed mental disorder, perhaps the subjects simply treated the experiment as a game. Whether the wage was high or low, subjects were experiencing a novel challenge and wanted to see how well they could perform. Under this interpretation, overearning is no more irrational than playing a video game; why pound your fingers on a controller and stare at a screen for no pay?

Although we may feel uncomfortable admitting it, play is pervasive in life, even for adults. For instance, motorists sometimes drive around looking for cheaper gas when the cost of gas used in the search outweighs the likely savings. They might defend this behavior by claiming that they don't want to be gouged or that they want to punish greedy gas station owners. But unless they spend resources punishing profiteers in general, this does not seem to be their real concern. Couldn't consumers simply see gas station owners as adversaries in a game? Why should we question the judgment of consumers sacrificing efficient consumption so they can win? While it may be tempting to suggest more efficient solutions to someone hunting for cheaper gas, fixing her own car, or knitting his own sweater, doing so would be inconsiderate. If they wanted to think harder about the obvious inefficiencies, they would already have done so.

The same logic applies when, rather than fighting an adversary, we're helping someone in need. Some people give money to panhandlers—occasionally. No one can argue that this is the most efficient way to reduce poverty. This capricious gesture cannot be cast in any cogent way as a purposeful optimization of fixed preferences. We may tell ourselves that charity will lead to rewards in this life (if we buy into the Western take on karma) or the afterlife (if we believe in a God who actively judges human affairs). Yet given that other types of charity would be more effective, these justifications amount to nothing more than efforts to defend our self-image as rational. Whatever we may tell ourselves, this spontaneous act of mercy is for-itself.

PART II

Belief

The conviction of the necessity of one's convictions survives the most strenuous opposition and extensive contradiction . . . Since the self, even as it is transformed by its interactions with the world, also transforms how that world seems to itself, its system of self-securing is not thereby "unhinged" nor is it "corrected" by cosmopolitanism. Rather, in enlarging its view "from China to Peru," it may become all the more imperialistic, seeing in every horizon of difference new peripheries of its own centrality.

—BARBARA HERRNSTEIN SMITH, *Contingencies of Value*

3
Acting in Character

One sick person self-medicates with natural remedies, while another strictly follows the doctor's orders. A third rejects treatment altogether and relies on prayer. All three believe they are doing the right thing.

Faith in natural remedies may stem from deeply held counterculture principles, mystical beliefs in the body's self-healing powers, or distrust of the medical establishment. This faith may have been reinforced by a personal experience in which alternative medicine seemed to work. Conviction in modern medicine goes together with an opposite constellation of beliefs: scientific evidence is the highest standard, and the system that generates this evidence and delivers therapies to patients can be trusted. And the third person, who believes events are in divine hands, might rely on the experience of previously answered prayers. She rejects the scientific method because she believes that God works in mysterious ways.

The diversity of opinion in the world is astonishingly vast—far vaster than we would expect if everyone used beliefs merely as instruments to maximize results. Rather than formulating hypotheses, then checking them against empirical evidence to ensure we adopt only the most accurate ones, we pick beliefs that appeal to us. Each of us grounds our beliefs in other beliefs we already hold and favors experiential knowledge over equally valid knowledge gained secondhand. We find ways to dismiss arguments to the contrary. As Walt Whitman observed, "Logic and sermons never convince."[1]

Before launching into the discussion, let's clarify our terms. We'll define beliefs as propositions that guide action and aren't necessarily true as a matter of logic, grammar, or common knowledge that no one can reasonably dispute. For our purposes, then, "$5 \times 7 = 35$," "bachelors are not married," and "the earth is bigger than the moon" are not beliefs. The realm of belief includes statements that could in principle be confirmed or refuted by evidence but where there is room to disagree. Examples of beliefs about treating illness are "herbal remedies work best," "only medicine approved by the FDA is to be trusted," and "prayer is the most effective." Beliefs are supported to some extent by data, but for most people that's not the only criterion—at least that's my strong belief and the premise of this chapter.

Acting in Character Is For-Itself

According to the rational choice model, individuals' actions are determined by their preferences and their resources, including financial wealth and human capital. Two rational, optimizing individuals with the same preferences and resources will make the same choices. Differences in risk aversion, from the standpoint of purposeful choice, can be accounted for as simply a matter of taste, that is, as further inputs into preferences. Expanding the model to incorporate behavioral biases allows for divergent courses of action if one person thinks more clearly than the other.

But in practice, people differ not only in their preferences and capacity to satisfy those preferences, but also in the beliefs they have formed. Beliefs take on a life of their own—they are more to us than tools to get ahead. They make up our identity.[2] We care about them. We want our beliefs to be consistent with each other and with our experience. We want to be able to defend our beliefs with reasons we can understand and remember, only gradually revising them over time based on reflection and experience. We try to act within those beliefs, sometimes at the expense of maximizing our preferences.

Holding onto beliefs and acting within them is not another kind of desire that we can evaluate and trade off when it serves our purposes. When we change our beliefs we change ourselves, triggering feedback into our preferences. Tenaciously maintaining beliefs must be understood as for-itself.

To see why, let's consider a woman who has lived in Texas all her life and thinks it's the best place on earth. When offered a two-year, high-paying job in New York City, though, she's tempted. She could earn enough to return to Texas and buy a ranch. But if she trades her cowboy boots for snow boots, jaywalks because she's now too impatient to wait for the light to change, and learns to be amused rather than repulsed when she sees rats chase each other in the subway tracks, soon she'll be a . . . New Yorker. As she comes to appreciate New York's charms, she may cease to believe all the wonderful things about Texas that defined her. When considering whether to take the job, she has to imagine what it would be like to give up her identity as a Texan. If she stays in New York for good, she'll have to think about the fact that the money she earns won't go so far. The move makes perfect sense if she can assure herself she'll come back to Texas with the loot as the same person who left. But that's not the way it works. She's got a decision to make. Purposeful choice, by itself, won't give her the answer.

And it's not just life-changing decisions, like whether to move from Texas to New York, that expose the limits of rational choice. Let's say the same woman is considering how to invest her savings. She doesn't like Wall Street or the idea of making money without doing work that feels real. She likes that the Texas economy depends on real things: oil, aeronautics, and agriculture. She grew up hearing how her family lost everything in 1929, so she doesn't invest in stocks. From my point of view, her investments will probably underperform, but who's to say?

One day, to everyone's surprise, she invests in a technology stock that she finds exciting. She took a rare leap outside her settled beliefs just like the characters in any narrative that holds our attention. But the characters can't leap too far or too often, or the plot would become incoherent. When we jump outside our beliefs, we are saying, in effect, "At this moment, my beliefs are no more compelling than this one-time act of will."

How Beliefs Are Formed

The American philosopher Charles Sanders Peirce outlined four routes to adopting a belief:

1. A new belief X is consistent with the things one already knows.
2. An authority to which one has committed says that X is so.
3. X is the style of thing that one is inclined to believe. In Peirce's words, X is "agreeable to reason."
4. A new belief X, when subjected to the scientific method, corresponds to data in the world.[3]

Loosely speaking, beliefs formed according to the first three routes allow us to build a coherent identity. Acting on settled beliefs, even ones that run contrary to empirical evidence, is not irrational but for-itself. In *Repetition*, Kierkegaard asks, "What would life be if there were no repetition? Who could want to be a tablet on which time writes something new every instant?"[4]

Rather than starting over, constantly reinventing ourselves in response to new data, we stick with who we are.

Only the fourth route is consistent with rational choice. Of course, a person solely interested in gratifying desires would incorporate the opinions of authorities to the extent that she trusted them to objectively convey valid information. She would dispassionately consider whether a new belief conflicted with existing beliefs, again as just more data. She would adopt new beliefs quickly if the preponderance of evidence favored a change.

In Peirce's outline, we care whether our beliefs are consistent in terms of logic and style. We are slow to depart from the existing beliefs that make up our character, even if those beliefs fail to hold up against new data. Couldn't this desire to act in character be incorporated into models of rational choice? Specifically, couldn't economists introduce a "belief-adjustment cost" or put a price on acting outside our beliefs? Let's consider what that modification would entail.

When we encounter data that conflict with our beliefs, we experience what Peirce calls "the irritation of doubt." We work to resolve that doubt by either modifying our beliefs to the minimum extent possible or explaining away the data. To even consider switching to a new belief, we would have to (1) imagine integrating that belief with our other beliefs and then (2) decide whether to switch. Not only does the first part of this undertaking come at a cost in terms of irritation, but it threatens to change us in ways we cannot anticipate, whether we adopt the new belief or not.

Another problem arises from actions that threaten to change beliefs in unpredictable ways. The Texan feared she might become a New Yorker in part because beliefs feed back into preferences. On whose behalf, then, do we choose? Our old familiar self or our partially new self? We are reluctant to change our beliefs to better satisfy the preferences of the person that those new beliefs would partially form, and with whom we share only a partial connection. Therefore we may choose not to evaluate the opposing belief at all and instead put on blinders. If doubt lingers, we can work to make existing beliefs feel rational—to "rationalize" them.

These sorts of considerations can't be modeled by rational choice theory unless that model includes a homunculus who sits on top of a person, controlling the adoption of beliefs and desires to form a new person whose desires can be gratified. We'd then arrive at yet another conundrum: sorting out what the homunculus was trying to achieve.

Some Consequences of Acting in Character

Now let's consider some practical consequences of the theory that people act in character rather than as robotic agents who merely calculate. I will take as axiomatic that people generally act on beliefs they feel entitled to hold and that commitment to these beliefs is for-itself. For-itself action can relate to a preexisting desire you pursue in your own way, even knowing that your way is inefficient. (For example, you'd like to be fashionably dressed, to make a positive impression. Yet you wear a ragged coat. Every single one of your friends tells you it's a mistake, but you answer, "I just like it, it's who I am.") Or it can be purely expressive (you wait in line at the polls to vote for a candidate who shares your beliefs even if your vote has no chance of swaying the election). The key premise is that acting in character on one's beliefs is not traded at a price for other types of gratification.

A person acting in character is not necessarily oblivious to incentives. If someone offered you enough money to switch to a better coat, you'd have your price. But so long as no external agents bribe you to change, you'll observe a sturdy attachment to certain beliefs. That is, you won't shift on the margin to a slightly more up-to-date coat if the cost goes down.

The two categories of action—purposeful and for-itself—compete to explain many phenomena, and it's not always easy to distinguish between them. Each offers its own account of the following ways we form beliefs and act on them.

Disregarding Expert Opinion

Why do people bother formulating their own opinions? I hold a few eccentric beliefs in areas where I'm far from expert. Do I know something that has eluded everyone else? Probably not. I recognize that this is strange, yet I'm utterly convinced and nothing is likely to shake those beliefs.

A PURPOSEFUL CHOICE INTERPRETATION

Rational people might discount an expert if they suspect she is selling something. Or the value of widely available advice may be competed away; if a food critic recommends a restaurant, then the restaurant might become crowded until the extra cost of waiting for a table equaled the value of the information in the review. Or an employee might rationally ignore an expert out of blame aversion; her boss could blame her for laziness if she relied on advice that turned out to be bad.

Various cognitive biases could further encourage obstinacy. According to behavioral economics, we overestimate our own abilities, seek out evidence that confirms our preconceptions, and are generally overconfident.

A FOR-ITSELF INTERPRETATION

We have a gift for dismissing those who disagree with us. Why else would we argue so passionately that experts have missed a point that is obvious to us? We question their motives, or if their motives withstand scrutiny, question their competence. We reflexively perceive our own opinions as derived from objective evidence and opposing views as suspect. Defying experts is a for-itself act of will. If we adopted new beliefs every time an expert instructed us to, our identities would be shifting, fragile, and incoherent.

Clinging to False Beliefs

It's unusual for people to change their minds and doubly unusual for them to change their minds quickly. According to legend, Keynes quipped, "When the evidence changes, I change my mind. What do you do, sir?"[5] But this was rhetoric to intimidate adversaries into coming around to his side. Like most everyone, Keynes held reasonably consistent, cohesive views his entire life.

In one of the prototypical problems for social scientists studying the persistence of false beliefs, some people continue to insist that childhood vaccinations for mumps, measles, and rubella (MMR) cause autism, even though the single study that made this claim was long ago discredited. When confronted with the data, rebellious parents refuse to change their minds. In a large randomized trial, doctors tried four interventions. In the first, they explained that no evidence links the MMR vaccine to autism. In the second, they explained the dangers of measles, mumps, and rubella. In the third, they recounted the story of an infant whose life was imperiled by measles. Finally, they showed images of children sick from a disease the vaccine would have prevented. Compared to a control group, none of the subjects grew more willing to vaccinate their children, and graphic images of sick children actually strengthened parents' belief that the MMR vaccine causes autism.[6]

A PURPOSEFUL CHOICE INTERPRETATION

A professed belief in the side effects of vaccinations may be a convenient excuse for parents with a firm grasp on their self-interest. The benefit of a vaccination is partly to protect one's child from disease but mostly to keep one's child from spreading it to others. Vaccination is an essentially altruistic act. A selfish person who cared only about her own child's welfare might prefer that all other children get vaccinated instead, sparing her the inconvenience. Or the failure of these interventions could be attributed to cognitive bias. The subjects might fall prey to the "hostile attribution bias," a kind of generalized paranoia, and conclude that the interventions are a trick by pharmaceutical companies.

A FOR-ITSELF INTERPRETATION

A person committed to the idea that pharmaceutical companies behave recklessly might welcome a study purporting to link autism and vaccination, however flawed. Even after the study was discredited, such a person might defend it and dismiss the countervailing evidence as a business-led conspiracy. Rumors might circulate of dark forces suppressing studies that confirmed a statistical link. To such a person, the story of one child who showed signs of autism after being vaccinated would be persuasive. She just doesn't like vaccines.

Favoring Experiential Knowledge

In ordinary conversation, experience is the gold standard of justification. I was there. I saw it with my own eyes. It takes a lot of theory and a lot of data to defeat that authority. Politicians embellish their humble origins as if experience with poverty gave them special insight into policies to help the poor. Soldiers believe one has to be a veteran to run the armed forces; it's not enough to be a military historian, no matter how much you know.

A PURPOSEFUL CHOICE INTERPRETATION

There are several reasons to favor experiential knowledge, even if we care about knowledge only as a means to an end. First, it is often more reliable. When we hear about something second-hand, truth or completeness may have been degraded along the way, whether or not the distortions were intentional. Second, experiential knowledge is easier to remember. Psychologically, experience generates vivid memories that we retain more easily than information we read. Third, trying something is the most effective way of finding out what you don't know you don't know. As Mark Twain put it, "The person that had took a bull by the tail once had learnt sixty or seventy times as much as a person that hadn't."[7]

Let's say you heard about a ship setting sail with spare capacity. You might think about renting space on the ship cheaply and loading it with goods to be sold at its destination. You don't know much about shipping, so you read a book about it and discuss your plan with experts. But you won't pull the trigger. To act, you would need deeper experiential knowledge—the real stuff, the knowledge of particulars that can't be fully transferred by explicit instruction. You'd want to hang around ports to see what ships are like. You'd want to get to know people who'd made similar deals. Only this sort of experience yields the localized knowledge that economist Friedrich Hayek ascribed to the "man on the spot," as opposed to scientific knowledge that can be transmitted freely from person to person.[8]

A FOR-ITSELF INTERPRETATION

Experiential knowledge is central to for-itself behavior. Our identities are formed by what we learn this way.

Reacting to Extreme Unexpected Events

In the run-up to the financial crisis, the investment bank Lehman Brothers collapsed. After that, anything seemed possible. It was natural to ask, "If the venerable Lehman can fall virtually overnight, why not this extreme event or that one?" In the summer of 2009, I was discussing custody arrangements with an investor in my fund who worked at a public pension plan managing vast sums of money. The fund's assets were to be held in Bank of New York Mellon, custodian for around $25 trillion in assets, equivalent to half the capitalization of all the stock markets in the world.

We spent thirty minutes earnestly discussing the likelihood that Bank of New York Mellon would abscond with client assets like Lehman Brothers' London-based affiliate had, in what the bankruptcy judge called a "truly spectacular" failure to observe rules designed to protect investors.[9] I argued that a Lehman-style collapse of the bank could lead to a breakdown of civilized society and that, under such conditions, nothing would be safe.

As alarmist as this conversation might seem today, at the time it made sense. It was a kind of extreme caution in response to the discovery of a "black swan," the metaphor for something never seen before. To those afflicted with "black swanitis," black swans and white swans become equally probable, and even the smallest chance becomes entirely likely. This mindset can be purposeful or for-itself.

A PURPOSEFUL CHOICE INTERPRETATION

The appearance of a black swan shakes our confidence in our beliefs, so we proceed cautiously. Under ordinary circumstances we act according to David Hume's principle of induction, believing that the sun will rise every day because it always has. But in some cases, the routine can change, as it does for Bertrand Russell's chickens, who don't fear the farmer because he has treated them well in the past.[10] When the farmer shows up one morning and several chickens disappear, it still might not be clear that he will soon wring their necks. Yet a rational chicken should sense that something is afoot and, as a cautionary measure, retreat quietly to the back of the coop.

Inaction in response to disorientation may even have a biological basis. Evolutionary biologists have long speculated that depression could confer a survival advantage by prompting people to withdraw from failed projects. As Darwin himself argued, "Pain or suffering of any kind, if long continued, causes depression and lessens the power of action, yet it is well adapted to make a creature guard itself against any great or sudden evil."[11] If your life is a mess and everything you try goes wrong, rather than fixing it with incremental steps, you might need to shut down and reassess your strategy.

A FOR-ITSELF INTERPRETATION

A person might be able to profit from converting quickly to new beliefs suited to the post-black-swan environment, sure, but she'd feel more responsible adjusting slowly. Sometimes an extreme experience transforms us instantly, for better or worse. This, however, is so rare that it's mostly the purview of myth and literature—say, when Macbeth encounters the three spooky witches who prophesize his future and turn him into an ambition-crazed maniac. Among the most famous conversions is that of Saul of Tarsus on the road to Damascus. On his way to persecute followers of Jesus, he sees a vision and is struck blind by a great light. Three days later, he regains his sight and switches sides with a vengeance. Or how about Siddhartha? After leaving his father's palace, he encounters an old man, a diseased man, a decaying corpse, and a wandering monk. Overcome by the suffering he'd witnessed, he leaves his family to live as an ascetic, ultimately finding enlightenment and becoming the Buddha.

Whatever the reason—purposeful or for-itself—the cure for inaction in the face of sudden upheaval is time. For rational actors, the ground will eventually start to firm up again. Most of those with for-itself black swanitis will gradually reconstitute their beliefs to fit the new environment, while a few will act despite their uncertainty.

Stock-Picking and Identity

When I ask my students, "Of those who invest in the stock market, how many pick your own stocks?" hands shoot up. Next, I ask: "How many of you invest in a diversified portfolio, such as the S&P 500?" No hands. Finally, I ask: "How many of you know that a non-diversified portfolio conflicts with economic theory?" They all raise their hands and laugh.

My students are not alone in ignoring the precept that they can maximize return and minimize risk by holding a portfolio of assets that is diversified. Investors often diversify far less than the capital asset pricing model advises and overweight their portfolio toward their home country more than transaction costs alone can justify. This tendency is a notorious embarrassment to portfolio theory. But we need not resort to cognitive biases to account for it. The explanation lies in the importance of choice, whether or not that choice strictly maximizes profit.

Suppose people are drawn to four or five investments, based on admiration of certain companies, tips from friends, or trends they believe will benefit certain businesses. They talk about these investments with friends and feel connected to companies in which they own only a small share. They tend to pick stocks from their home country because they identify more readily with its fortunes. (It's unlikely that retail investors have an informational advantage in their home country. If it were that easy, hedge funds would station analysts in every country.) Even investors who do diversify with mutual funds want to at least choose which fund and the timing of the investment. Long before the inventors of portfolio theory, Harry Markowitz and William F. Sharpe, were born, Kierkegaard scorned the person who "acts as shrewdly in life as the financiers who put their resources into widely diversified investments in order to gain on one if they lose on another—in short, he is not a knight [of faith]."[12] Although gaining on one to counterbalance losses on another is a sound strategy for minimizing risk, we sometimes want to stand by our own leaps of faith.

People who identify with their personal investments tend to shun companies that offend them. There's little evidence that selling shares of a company with rough labor practices deprives it of capital or influences its conduct. Selling is instead a personal decision, rationalized with specious economic logic. I am too steeped in economic theory to delude myself: divesting of any particular stock would be no more than symbolic. Still, I wouldn't invest in a tobacco company—I prefer not to make money from selling cigarettes and am not sacrificing much return. At the same time, I acknowledge that some other investor will buy the shares I don't and the amount of smoking in the world will remain undiminished.

Just as individuals express themselves through personal investments, groups can express themselves collectively through divestment. The Government Pension Fund of Norway decided to sell its shares of companies involved in the production of fossil fuels. To the extent that Norway's divestment temporarily reduces share prices below their fundamental value, another investor who is untroubled by such matters will buy. Even if activists could permanently depress the share values of oil giants by a small amount, the effect on the companies' ability to raise capital would be minuscule. It's a lot of fuss for little substantive impact, or none at all. Even so, divestment was approved by a democratically elected parliament and expresses the will of the Norwegian people.

Investments are ultimately more than a means of maximizing wealth; they also allow us to express who we are and what we value while undertaking an unpredictable adventure.

4

Making Money in Financial Markets

Anatomy of a Leap

I do not believe in astrology. It does not fit with my preexisting beliefs, and no authority I recognize would instruct me to believe in it. As for matching the facts, I'm not impressed: proponents of astrology can offer only anecdotes. But I'm sure I'd be unable to sway an astrologer who is impressed by the times the stars predicted the future and brushes off the times they did not. For such a person, astrology satisfies all four of Peirce's criteria. For me, it satisfies none. The astrologer and I must agree to disagree.

I do believe that there are times when a trader can expect to make money in competitive financial markets, but not in ways that can be codified. I'm drawn to arguments that appeal to subtle epistemic considerations, like those we'll encounter in the following pages. I have spent enough of my life as a trader and in the company of traders to believe that any convincing theory must address why, if markets are so efficient, these seemingly rational people spend so much time trying to beat them. The belief that some people and some institutions can make money fits with my other beliefs. I have a strong impression that it fits the data but, like an astrologer, I draw my evidence from anecdotes. Sometimes people make money, sometimes they lose, yet I hold that some of the winners reasonably and responsibly knew that they were likely to win.

I can't subject my belief to rigorous statistical tests. If there were a testable rule for beating the market, everyone would already know it and it would cease to work. Instead, there are lots of rules, many conflicting, and knowing which ones to follow is the whole game. Beating the market should not be easy. Trades hide in the world. I believe I know an opportunity when I see one, but I sometimes turn out to be wrong. Opportunities arise sporadically and almost always involve a unique encounter with the unknown. Investors must be willing to take an out-of-character leap.

The purposeful choice model—which presents people as machines that process the sort of information that machines can understand—is good enough for many problems, but not for explaining much of what is interesting in financial markets. Although the overarching pursuit of profit is purposeful, purposeful choice cannot model out-of-character trading and investing. You can't "make your own luck" by working longer and harder, undergoing apprenticeships and academic training, or steeling yourself to take a risk—although none of that would hurt. Because this type of investing involves unique one-time events, each leap into the unknown draws only partially on tried-and-true rules. It necessarily takes you from the realm of signals, risk, and reward into the murkier realm of hunches, judgment, and anxiety. Out-of-character trading and investing must, then, be understood as for-itself.

The Efficient Market Hypothesis

It is often said that the key to making money is knowing things that other people don't know. A corollary to this maxim is the textbook definition of the efficient market hypothesis: markets are efficient if prices reflect all publicly available information. That is, no one can expect to beat the market unless they know more than the public. The standard approach to testing market efficiency follows from this definition. It assumes that information comes in one variety and that it is objective and accessible to everyone. It allows for uncertainty but assumes that risk can be modeled.

Since the 1960s, detractors of the efficient market hypothesis have identified potential anomalies in the data that a savvy trader could exploit, and defenders have counterattacked with one of three claims: (1) The detractors looked at hundreds of possible anomalies and only published one—even if markets are perfectly unpredictable, some patterns will appear by chance, (2) There's a flaw in the detractors' analysis (for instance, transaction costs would chew up apparent profit or the securities were not really available at the published price), or (3) Any above-market returns can be attributed to risk, since the payoff is positively correlated with other financial assets or human capital. In return, detractors point to alleged cognitive biases, such as loss aversion, as the reason that money-making opportunities persist. Defenders then respond that some people may be biased some of the time, but even a small number of arbitrageurs can force the market to its proper level.[1]

I am neither in favor of the efficient market hypothesis, nor against it. I am against the way it frames the debate: it mischaracterizes markets by ignoring different ways of possessing information. The standard definition of efficient markets assumes that information consists of no more than generic signals that tell the receiver something about the world. Thus, the informed trader, by effort, luck, or cheating, can acquire a superior signal. But the true key to making money is knowing things in *ways* that other people do not. It is a deep understanding of crucial information like that held by Hayek's man on the spot that leads to profitable action.

To act on such opportunities, even the best-informed investor must take a leap. Because a unique event cannot be understood as an abstraction to which simple rules apply, investing with a likelihood of beating the market requires, as Richard Zeckhauser argues, an engagement with the "unknown and unknowable."

Zeckhauser tells a story about the economist David Ricardo, who bought British government bonds before the Battle of Waterloo on a hunch that the Duke of Wellington and his Prussian allies would defeat Napoleon. What was the probability of such a victory? What previous battle could have served as a comparison? It was a river that the world would step in only once. Ricardo made his bet and won big.[2]

If pressed for a reason, Ricardo might have argued that British government bonds offered a high potential reward for the risk. On the surface, this looks like a clear proposition, similar to "investors can achieve higher expected returns and less risk with a diversified portfolio than with a portfolio of a few randomly selected stocks" or that "stocks that pay high dividends generate, on average, higher total returns than stocks that pay no dividends." But unlike Ricardo's proposition, these two statements can be tested against data and proven true or false. Suppose France had won, or Britain had won but the bonds didn't appreciate as Ricardo expected. The resulting loss might be chalked up to bad luck, although in this context it would be difficult to distinguish between bad luck and bad judgment. The conditions that spurred Ricardo to buy the bonds were deeply ambiguous. They had never arisen before and would never arise again.

Along with engaging with the unknown and unknowable, Zeckhauser proposes two further necessary conditions for beating the market: (1) The opportunity is available only to those with a particular complementary capability, such as the ability to develop an office building, and (2) It is unlikely that the party on the other side of the transaction is better informed. He also lists freedom from "blame aversion" as a likely condition—an investor who isn't subject to second-guessing from her boss is more likely to beat the market.

I believe Zeckhauser is right in most cases about complementary skills (although there are exceptions, which I will discuss later). He's also right, of course, that traders can't succeed if they are criticized the moment they show a loss. "Blame aversion," though, is a superficial term to describe the imperfect communication between a principal and an agent when the agent contends with unique events. "Aversion" suggests a psychological phenomenon, but these barriers to communication would remain even if everyone in the decision chain mastered their biases.

Zeckhauser's idea of engagement with unknowable events is akin to what I call "acting out of character." That doesn't mean acting without principle or in direct conflict with one's defining qualities, but that the engagement is not rule-based or systematic. Because this conduct doesn't belong to the purposeful realm, it must be for-itself. Above-market returns can be made when the agent abandons fixed procedures, considers the particular situation on its own merits, for itself, and leaps.

For-itself investing has always been and will always be in short supply because of the anxiety it entails—people can only bear so much, and institutions are not built for it. When we confront a one-time event without the guidance of familiar rules, we're on our own. This indeterminacy and freedom and the ensuing sense of isolation and responsibility can give rise to dread. Adam Smith expressed it perfectly when he suggested that "*anxious* vigilance" was the defining quality of a good manager, who must often operate under novel and uncertain conditions, doing that which can't be transcribed into rules and delegated.[3] Anyone who spots an opportunity to buy or sell because prices have drifted from their fundamental value places herself in opposition to the prevailing canon. It is hard to say, "This will make money," when everyone has been taught that making above-market returns is impossible. It feels daring at best, uneducated at worst.

If you go against the grain, pitching to an investment committee a deal that's similar to one that failed in the past, saying "this time feels different," less sporting colleagues are likely to haul out the cliché falsely attributed to Einstein: "The definition of stupidity [or insanity] is to try the same thing over again and expect a different result." If others have lost fortunes in certain securities, why should it be different for you? If you try in spite of these warnings and fail, then according to the cliché, you are stupid or insane. And since markets are efficient, it was foolish to even entertain the idea that you might beat them.

But that argument is too simplistic. It's possible to hold simultaneously the views that markets are efficient and agents are rational, and that at least some investors can expect returns beyond what they might earn with a diversified portfolio of stocks. To realize these returns, an investor must act out of character on an informed hunch. For-itself trading falls beyond, and so reveals a limit to, market efficiency.

Institutional Investing

Let's start by taking a look at credit markets that are the domain of public and private pension funds, sovereign wealth funds, insurance companies, university endowments, and other institutional investors. How can a hierarchical group undertake a leap that hinges on personal beliefs formed on the front lines? And having taken the leap, how can it hang on through signs of trouble?

From a trading standpoint, institutions differ from individuals in two ways: their resources give them access to esoteric and illiquid markets, and they have governance structures that prevent individuals from misusing resources. These governance structures naturally treat all trades as purposeful and none as for-itself, leaving institutional investors ill-equipped to engage with one-time events.

Suppose you're a salesperson at an investment bank. An infrastructure project has unexpectedly run out of money due to mismanagement. A new investor with $250 million could seize the project from its distressed owners before it files for bankruptcy. With only one week to close the deal, the new investor would have to skip most of the usual due diligence. The decision requires speed, trust, and judgment. As the salesperson, are you going to show the deal to the California Public Employees' Retirement System (CalPERS) or to a billionaire tech entrepreneur?

At best, the CalPERS managers would say, "Yes, it's probably a great deal but we don't have time for approvals," or "Yes, it's probably a great deal but we have no bucket in which to put it." The billionaire tech entrepreneur, sniffing a profit, will pounce.

Institutional investors manage funds more or less in accordance with a common formula. A board of trustees approves a policy that a chief investment officer (CIO) then implements. The policy usually splits the fund into "buckets," "sectors," or "asset classes." Sectors can include domestic public equity, global equity, credit, illiquid credit, private equity, cash, absolute return (hedge funds), and the like.

The CIO assigns specialists to look after each sector. Equity managers handle equity; credit managers handle credit. For the public equities sector, some CIOs farm out stock selection to outside managers, and others invest passively in an index fund to hold down costs. Often a risk management department monitors the entire portfolio. In the case of pension funds, the board pays attention to how assets match liabilities to pensioners.

Funds define risk mainly in terms of exposure to the market as a whole. The term "alpha" is supposed to describe the expected return beyond what can be explained by correlation with the stock market. When trustees want to take on more risk, they dial up allocations to volatile investments, such as stocks. Some might decide to shift cash into hedge funds while preserving their stock market exposure. Or they might ask the CIO to deliberately "overweight" a sector or subsector, such as growth stocks.

All this is predicated on the idea that risk can be modeled and aggregated. Few big institutions take risks by departing from conventional decision-making.

For-itself theory suggests an alternate approach: lining up investment propositions on the continuum of knowability. The most senior, most trustworthy individuals—those the board deems to have the keenest judgment—would deal with the murkiest opportunities and operate under the least oversight. They would be empowered to deal with each unique opportunity on its own merits and evaluated over a long-term horizon in a governance structure that understands that not all decisions can be justified using the standard metrics and terminology.

To enjoy the benefits of for-itself investing, an institution would, of course, have to tolerate occasional losses that look foolish after the fact. And the people closest to the decision would really feel the sting. Whether a fund manager must apologize to the CIO or the CIO must apologize to the trustees of a pension fund, there would be no theory or data to fall back on. In for-itself investing, individuals must bear responsibility for losses.

Individual Investing

Back before the financial crisis knocked the stuffing out of individual investors, a security guard at my office building often asked me for stock tips. He was a frustrated day trader. When he won, he felt on top of the world, like he'd found the magic formula. When his winning streak came to an end, he'd reproach himself for missing some signal or other. I'd congratulate him on good days and commiserate on bad ones, but he wanted more. He thought I was holding out on him. Finally, late one evening, I gave in: "Okay, I'll tell you the secret."

Boy, did I have his attention.

Then I explained, "There is no secret. There is no way for you to compete with Brad," the trader at our fund. "He has technology, information, low trading costs, and twenty-five years of experience. If there's an opportunity, he'll take advantage of it before you possibly could. And even Brad wins only 52 percent of the time. There are no patterns—any patterns you think you've discovered are illusions. This is nothing personal. No one in your position, no matter how smart or hard working, has a chance of beating Brad's record."

That guard left my building years ago and, for all I know, he made some lucky trades, retired to a tropical island, and laughs at me every day. But I doubt it. He liked to read books on investing, and wherever he is, I hope he's reading this one, because I've rethought my response a little. There is one arena in which an individual investor might get ahead: for-itself investing.

The nature of for-itself investing gives individual investors one clear advantage over institutions. While someone trading with her own money lacks the resources of an institution—she can't fund the development of a new drug from scratch or buy complex derivatives when everyone else is trying to sell—she can do as she likes. For-itself investing can't be boiled down to a set of rules or achieved through a mechanically applied procedure. It requires a leap outside of settled beliefs. The independent individual can more readily take such a leap.

I don't mean short-term trading, which comes with high transaction costs that make it almost impossible for individuals to compete with professionals. Nor am I talking about trading based on market patterns or trends, since they don't really exist. Even the concept of a "bull market" is unfounded. Stocks that go up one month are just as likely to go up (the trend continues) or down (the trend reverses or "corrects") the next. The phrase "the stock market is going up" uses the wrong verb tense: it *went* up. Stock prices aren't physical objects—they don't have momentum. If the market were going up, arbitrageurs would take advantage of that fact and drive it immediately to its destination.

Successful investing has to be more than following rules. Any set of rules that led to effortless profits would immediately be arbitraged away. Consider the advice to "be contrarian" or "zig when others zag," which is so conventional that it has become impossible to execute. If everyone decides to be contrarian, then everyone's the same, and no one is contrarian. Rather than contrarian, thinking must be *independent*.

Individuals, though unable to beat hedge funds at short-term trading, can be more independent than any institution possibly could. An individual can act on a whim, without explaining herself to peers, managers, regulators, the press, or investors. She enjoys a close connection to her own money and long-term freedom from blame. The hedge fund manager with tentative control over other people's money can't compete with the coordination that takes place within a single mind. And while the fund manager might be pressured to fold on an investment that started out poorly, an individual can hold on indefinitely.

According to legend, in 1889, one of Van Gogh's sunflower paintings sold for $125. The same painting sold in 1987 for around $36 million. This story is a staple of introductory finance courses to illustrate the wonders of compound interest. The annual rate of return works out to 13.7 percent, less than you might have guessed. The lesson is supposed to be: a plausible annual return can eventually turn into a mighty sum if you let it compound for a long time. But the real lesson is that 13.7 percent is a very high annual return to achieve year after year. In my more successful investments, I stayed on my toes, mined some vein I'd discovered, and kept it up for what felt like a long time— a few years. It's amazing when an individual (or an institution that consists of a chain of individuals) can stay on her toes for decades, never calcifying or leaning on rules, and continually unearth unique opportunities.

In a sense, the Van Gogh painting is not one investment, but many. Each year, the owner has to choose not to sell it when the price rises. If we imagine it is held by one family the entire time, the heirs must decide to keep the painting rather than cash in. At various junctures, the owner has to make a for-itself leap: look at the painting, think about selling, look at it again, and finally decide to hold. Only when we hear the story summarized and abstracted from temptations on the ground does it sound miraculous.

In addition to holding on for a long time, the lone individual can take for-itself action even when the evidence is scanty or ambiguous—it's her own money, after all—while a fund manager rarely can. Individuals also have an obvious informational advantage in certain situations, such as investing in single-family residential real estate. In your own neighborhood, you are literally the man (or woman) on the spot. You can invest by buying a larger home than you require or by buying property to rent out.

Whatever investments you choose, even if you're a professional trader, there will be moments when it hurts. There remains no such thing as a free lunch. All I can offer is an attitude, a few tips, and a theoretical framework. But I wouldn't rule out the possibility that individuals can systematically make money in even the most competitive, liquid markets. The three years I traded on my own illustrate this point.

I started trading futures contracts for my own account after leaving my job at the Dai-Ichi Kangyo Bank. My first trade was a long position in May 2001, betting that the price of soybean futures would rise. I'm no expert in commodities and I'd never seen a soybean plant up close. Yet I knew that at a price of $4.28, farmers would lose $1.00 per bushel. Moreover, the market had ground steadily lower. I guessed that uninformed traders following what they believed to be a "trend" were depressing the price.

Speculators who'd bought at higher prices probably had to sell when their losses mounted to levels greater than they could tolerate. In trader jargon, they were "stopped out." But I could hold out as long as necessary because it was my own money. I even left room to buy more if prices fell. As it turned out, I never had a chance to add to my position: soybean prices rose and I sold my contract a month later at a profit.

My second trade was in October 2001, in a market where I had plenty of experience. I shorted five-year Treasury-note futures, betting the price would go down. Although I've long forgotten my logic for this trade, I bought back the futures in November after interest rates rose and prices for Treasuries fell.

For the third trade, also in October 2001, I bought soybeans again and sold a few weeks later at a profit. The fourth was a purchase of cotton, which I noticed had fallen below 30 cents per bushel. This reminded me of a song from the 1960s in which Johnny Cash lamented, "cotton is down to a quarter a pound, I'm busted." The overall price level had quadrupled since he sang those lyrics, making the current price of cotton around 6 cents per pound in 1960 dollars. The straits of cotton farmers must have been truly dire. I suspected that, as with soybeans, trend-following traders had driven down the price. I bought futures at 29 cents and sold in November at 36.2 cents.

While my experiment in trading contradicts a narrow definition of market efficiency, it does illustrate an efficient market in human skill and effort: by devoting about 10 percent of the time

I'd formerly spent on my job, I earned about 10 percent of my former pay.

What advantages did I have over institutional investors? I wasn't trying to achieve any particular target return. I took small positions to avoid risking too much. I didn't try to live off the winnings. If there were no good trades to do, I didn't have to do anything. I kept the trades secret; unlike a trader at a bank, I was free from worrying about how they might look to my boss or the risk management department. But that secrecy didn't make me a rogue trader—I can't be a rogue to myself! I had one more significant advantage: I had ridden the roller coaster enough times to develop some self-awareness. I didn't panic or despair when losing or become exuberant and rash when winning. Together, these factors allowed me to take for-itself action. Lots of people probably shared the intuition that soybean prices were unsustainably low, but I was in a position to act.

Although these trades were accompanied by Adam Smith's "anxious vigilance" to some degree, it took a bet on a wind farm to bring home the full (and sometimes grueling) implications of a for-itself leap under novel and uncertain conditions.

Thanet Offshore Wind: A Big Leap

There is a sentiment among traders that it's a bad omen to win on your first trade. Early success can go to your head and foster an unhealthy lack of caution. I know the truth of this sentiment because when our fund first stumbled into wind energy, we started out winning. In 2005, we were analyzing a transaction tied to a bank's loans to German wind farms, not such a departure from our normal business. But then we decided that instead of insuring loans, we'd rather own the wind farms themselves. Using money from our funds and debt from a security backed by the wind farms, we took a leap. We figured that investors would appreciate the lack of correlation between their other assets and wind farm returns, which depend largely on how hard the wind blows.

In late 2006, after construction was completed and the financing was in place, we sold the wind farms to a public company in the United Kingdom. So far, so good. We'd built enough wind farms to power 300,000 homes when the wind was blowing full blast and turned a solid profit in short order.

Then the wind changed direction.

In August 2007, we bought the rights to build a three-hundred-megawatt project, Thanet Offshore Wind, in the Thames Estuary. If constructed, it would be the largest offshore wind farm in the world. We had never built a wind farm that size but, as my partner Johan Christofferson and I said to ourselves, neither had anyone else. So we were, no question, acting out of character. (I should add that Johan and I don't think of ourselves as thrill-seeking daredevils, an impression you might get from reading the rest of this story. We enjoyed working at a Japanese bank where the highest praise was to call a colleague "reliable." Thanet was a gigantic break from the orderly lives we normally live.) We knew that in addition to the risks we'd identified, we would encounter unforeseeable risks once the project was under way, but we also calculated our expected returns with a large margin for error.

Of course, our leap was preceded by analysis. The site, in the Thames River Basin, could not be beat: it was sixty miles from the center of London and one of the windiest locations in the world suitable for offshore wind development. Auspiciously—or so we thought—we were able to buy the project company for what we believed to be a bargain price. Because of our winning track record and enthusiasm for Thanet, we were able to raise the money for the first phase of construction. What could go wrong?

Turns out, plenty. First, the prices of steel, copper, and oil surged. Wind farm foundations and towers are made of steel, and the cables that export the electricity to shore are made of copper. The spike in oil prices stimulated offshore drilling, raising demand for the specialized installation vessels that we needed to construct Thanet. Higher power prices boosted demand for turbines, and Vestas, our Danish supplier, raised its price by 30 percent. The project was growing more expensive by the day.

Delays set in. One of our barges capsized. A small airport in Kent, England, claimed that Thanet would interfere with its radar and demanded compensation in the form of extravagant new equipment. The fishermen's association tried to hold us up, claiming that it, too, needed compensation, even though the project was far out to sea, the cables would be buried deep underground, and the footprint of the towers was inconsequential.

I was nervous. In March 2008, Bear Stearns collapsed, and the financial crisis deepened. By June, I had a constant worry in the pit of my stomach. So we decided to get out while the getting was good. We hired an investment bank to put Thanet back on the market in early summer 2008. We received three nonbinding bids from credible buyers, any one of which would have delivered a spectacular profit. We went with the highest bidder, Iberdrola Renovables Energía, the Spanish electric utility. Iberdrola assigned a large deal team to the project, hired technical advisers, and engaged outside counsel. Senior members of the deal team canceled their summer vacations to close Thanet on September 4. Iberdrola was doing everything expected from a buyer, but it wasn't calming me down.

In late August, Iberdrola informed us that it wanted all documentation completed two weeks before funds were to flow. We moved the closing date from September 4 to September 30 to accommodate internal approvals within Iberdrola. The new date presented us with a serious challenge, since payments were due to various suppliers, such as Vestas, which was expecting a down payment of €125 million on September 6. Iberdrola contacted several of the affected suppliers directly to explain that the delay had resulted from its internal procedures and that it was committed to the September 30 close. All suppliers agreed to the revised terms except Vestas, which wanted €10 million for the delay. Otherwise, Vestas said, it would begin selling turbine slots to onshore projects.

In September, we negotiated the remaining contracts to Iberdrola's satisfaction. We persuaded some contractors to continue working and others to delay enforcement on sizeable obligations—the Belgian manufacturers of the steel foundations were owed €46.5 million but agreed to continue rolling 50,000 tons so that installation could start in December. Johan and I put most of our own money into the project to keep it afloat a few more days. What else could we do?

Then came the collapse of Lehman Brothers on September 15. My overall terror that day was heightened by fear for this deal. On the afternoon of Friday, September 26, we were informed that Iberdrola's CEO wanted to postpone the deal due to market conditions. The following Tuesday morning, he came to London to negotiate. We struck a revised deal, with our fund leaving its money in the project alongside Iberdrola's. The new closing date was set as Tuesday, October 7. Between Friday, October 3, and Tuesday, October 7, the S&P 500 fell 9.4 percent, leaving Iberdrola in no position to announce a project that would ultimately cost €1 billion. It walked away for good, as was its legal right. I was angry at the time but don't blame Iberdrola now. Its stock price had fallen precipitously with the rest of the renewable energy market. With commodities collapsing, a recession imminent, and credit vanishing, the Thanet project was no longer a prize.

Our secured loan was in default. Payments to about twenty suppliers, including Vestas, were overdue. The directors of Thanet worried that they might have a personal legal obligation to put the company in bankruptcy. No fresh money was in sight. Similar projects around the world, including other offshore wind farms in the works, simply shut down.

We asked the suppliers to continue working even though we couldn't pay them. We pleaded with the lender not to foreclose. Johan and I had to personally guarantee that the lawyers would be paid, risking everything, including our homes. DKB, the Japanese bank where we'd worked, was like a Disney movie by comparison—no matter what happened, it couldn't get too bad because the head office in Tokyo would always bail us out. And if the bank ever got into real trouble, the Japanese government would step in. But this time, it was just us facing the abyss.

If all the stakeholders—suppliers, lenders, advisers—played along, we all had a chance. If any one of them tried to enforce its rights and jump in front of other creditors in line, everyone would lose. It was a twenty-dimensional game of prisoner's dilemma.

My morning ritual after the Iberdrola deal broke down began with a call from the CEO of Vestas. "Richard," he would say, "I can't satisfy my board with talk." "Anders," I would answer, "if I had money, I would send it to you." These exchanges were always polite. "Sorry if the tone above seems hard or rude, this is not the intention, but it is a fact," he emailed. "Trouble is the common denominator of living," I reminded him, quoting Kierkegaard, his fellow Dane. As my day wore on, however, Thanet stakeholders, including disgruntled investors, would call, and interactions became less civil.

But while our conversations were tense, the investors were somewhat placated by the fact that Johan and I always took their calls, and that we were at risk of being wiped out personally when the Thanet sale imploded at the end of September. The UK Energy Ministry helped by encouraging suppliers to cooperate. Ultimately, the stakeholders hung on. Even the Belgian foundries kept working. I don't know how they paid for the steel. Probably the same way we paid them—with promises we hoped we'd be able to keep.

After Iberdrola backed out and threw the project into disarray, things got personal. Holding it together was not a task we could delegate. There was no chance of any outcome besides losing our shirts—the only real question was, how badly. We had dragged vendors and creditors into a giant mess and spent every day persuading stakeholders to give us another stay of execution. Some of them, by giving us a break, were acting out of character. On paper, we probably didn't look like a good bet. But we were good at begging.

A Swedish state-owned utility finally bought Thanet in mid-November. The offshore wind supply chain soaked up the utility's money like a desert in a rainstorm. The vendors and creditors were all paid in full. A little bit was left over for our investors, though not enough to recover our investment.

What did I learn from this experience? Maybe it's simple: not to have bad luck. If commodity prices hadn't zoomed up when they did, we would have been in stronger shape. If Lehman had collapsed six months earlier, before we spent so much money on Thanet, we could have delayed construction until markets recovered. If Lehman had collapsed three weeks later, our sale to Iberdrola would have closed, and we would have made a fortune. But when an investor asks me this question, answering in terms of luck feels disrespectful.

I doubt we'll try a project this risky again, but not because the experience taught us to avoid risk. The common expression "it took a lot out of me" feels about right. Stepping outside my beliefs, subjecting them to harsh reality, and settling back down again—there's only so much of that I can do. Even if I took a prudent risk and investors knew what they were getting into, I could still end up harming people who trusted me. My remorse shaped a new belief—that the emotional strain of risking other people's money to this extent is hard to bear, no matter how willingly they invest. Now that I have felt what that emotional strain is like, I know myself better. I handled that one harrowing episode and a few others like it, but that's enough. Since Thanet, our fund has stuck largely to our European credit business.

Construction of Thanet finished in 2010. Despite cost overruns, it is on track to deliver 8 to 10 percent annual returns for its new owners, including revenues from renewable subsidies. That's not far below what we projected back in 2007, even though power prices have fallen significantly.

I have little taste for inspirational stories of entrepreneurs who failed at one business after another, dusted themselves off, learned from their mistakes, and eventually hit it big. Sure, it ends well for the entrepreneur, but what about all the stakeholders—the employees, vendors, investors—the first few times around? Where is their happy ending? My colleagues and I take a small measure of satisfaction in knowing that Thanet was ultimately built, but we must live with the fact that we lost other people's money as well as our own.

Although I did once catch a glimpse of Thanet out of an airplane window, I have never been to visit it.

5

For-Itself Decision-Making within a Group

Let's revisit the impasse between the entrepreneur and the venture capitalist from Chapter 2. The entrepreneur walks into the office of the venture capitalist (VC) to ask for money to bring a new product to market. According to the entrepreneur's business plan, the product will take one year to develop. In the second year, her base case predicts revenues of $2 million, and her worst-case scenario predicts revenues of $1 million. The entrepreneur believes her product will generate these revenues if the VC gives her the money. She knows she's right. Her belief is based on first-hand encounters with the market she plans to address. Her actions confirm the strength of this belief—she has committed all her savings and exhibits an entrepreneur's customary zeal.

After reviewing the business plan and meeting with the entrepreneur, however, the VC estimates that the product will take at least three years to develop and will probably fail. The VC knows this. Her belief is based on experience with entrepreneurs and their business plans. (The VC will not tell the entrepreneur exactly what she thinks to avoid insulting her. It would be an "insult" rather than a "disagreement" because the entrepreneur's beliefs are personal.)

What the VC knows and what the entrepreneur knows cannot both be true. No one will ever discover the truth—if the entrepreneur gets the money and succeeds (or fails), maybe she was just lucky (or unlucky). Nothing either side can say will change the other's mind.[1]

As the unfortunate entrepreneur illustrates, one person's belief cannot automatically translate into a second person's belief, no matter how strongly held. Her efforts are impeded by a lack of common experience and the rigidities intrinsic to belief formation. The difficulty of transmitting a belief is particularly acute when that belief is about a proposed for-itself leap into the unknown. In business and investing, such beliefs are the most important to communicate—if any profitable course of action can be broken down into readily transmittable rules, odds are it's already been arbitraged away. Investors seem to be aware of this on some level. They say things like, "It's not risky for you but it is for me." It's an acknowledgment that the promoter of the deal has a kind of understanding that can't be fully shared.

This difficulty is compounded when many individuals must

be convinced, making it a great obstacle to for-itself institutional investing. It's a mistake to anthropomorphize institutions as if they could coordinate on a common belief or share information from a common perspective. Consider a hedge fund that specializes in structured credit and seeks to raise money from a pension fund to buy complicated bonds. The following chain of people would need to go along: the hedge fund's managers, an analyst at the pension fund, the analyst's boss, and the pension fund's investment committee. And finally, the pension fund managers must consider how the investment would look to trustees and to federal regulators.

Working up the chain, each party is another step further removed from the detailed knowledge that made the hedge fund manager want to buy these bonds. Each link in the chain must establish belief in its own way in order to act responsibly. If the deal resembles one that lost money within recent memory, the pension fund's investment committee is unlikely to be persuaded by the argument "This time will be different."

Even when all the actors are perfectly rational, properly incentivized, and in control of their emotions, communication challenges on an institutional scale can cause markets to seize up. They certainly did during the financial crisis. The fall in asset prices could have been cushioned if the largest institutional investors had bought corporate bonds and mortgage-backed securities when others were selling. Immobility in the face of for-itself opportunity contributed to the run on the banks and elevated a weakness in the housing market into a crisis that tested nearly every financial institution in the world.

Rich family offices controlled by strong-willed individuals skilled in finance could theoretically have helped fill the void left by immobilized institutional investors. In my experience, some did. But many did not: the richer the family head becomes, the less interested she is in digging into the technical details that a person on the spot needs to know and that earned the fortune in the first place. And the larger family offices grow, the more they adopt the controls typical of institutional investors.

Applying Peirce's rules, we can see why institutional investors hesitated to buy low-priced, complex, illiquid bonds. The fourth, purposeful rule—one applies the scientific method; the belief corresponds to data in the world—couldn't justify these investments. There were no data on similar events because nothing like this had ever happened before. Many looked to the Great Depression for precedent, but conditions were so different back then (asset-backed securities hadn't even been invented) that it couldn't provide much guidance.

The rules I've categorized as for-itself—those that deal with acting in character —would have been equally useless:

1. *A new belief X is consistent with the things one already knows.* Senior executives started with the view that bonds like this were dangerous.
2. *An authority to which one has committed tells one that X is so.*

During the crisis, few authorities were to be trusted, and fewer still recommended fishing on the bottom in structured finance.

3. *X is the style of thing one is inclined to believe.* Most would be inclined to believe the opposite—that complex securities were "toxic."

Institutional investors had little reason to adopt new beliefs and even less to take for-itself, out-of-character leaps into complex asset-backed bonds. Even if a hedge fund manager could convince analysts at a pension fund through intensive interactions that this was the time to throw the rules aside, the analysts could not then transfer this belief and knowledge up through their governance structure. Under normal conditions, it's hard enough for institutions to coordinate on for-itself hunches, no matter how well-informed, well-intentioned, and clear-headed each individual may be. It's nearly impossible when investors are in the grip of black swanitis.

The Best Trade Ever

The reasons behind this near-impossibility dawned on me during the financial crisis, after making one of many pitches to try to raise money to take advantage of the bargains I saw.

I had just finished a presentation to the managers of an endowment fund in Nashville, Tennessee. It seemed like nothing I could say and no analysis I could present would convince them. In my colleague's opinion, "We could have levitated over the conference table and asked, 'How'd you like to tap into these powers?' We could have pointed at a chair and turned it into gold. They still wouldn't have invested."

I believed that values in credit markets were extraordinary. (Of course, some deals that appear lucrative from a distance are not; at the time I believed I knew which were which.) Yet I simply couldn't beam my beliefs into investors' heads. Gradually, I saw that investors' reluctance had little to do with the usual factors: aversion to risk, information asymmetries, aversion to blame, aversion to ambiguity, herd mentality, or irrational fear. Investors could not fully adopt my conviction about any given opportunity before it disappeared. They could not act on a hunch that I (and others) might just be right. To do so, an investor would have to suspend her belief in reasonably efficient markets—usually, low asset prices signify risk, but not in the collapsing markets of 2008. She would have to rely on experts to make sure she wasn't missing anything. She'd have to dismiss the surface resemblance between the investments I was proposing and discredited sectors such as subprime mortgages. Then she'd have to persuade her investment committee, which would, in turn, have to convince other committees up the chain. After all that, she might have to wait for years before my beliefs were justified.

I understood this disconnect after rereading, and finally appreciating, the story of the best speculative bet of all time. It wasn't some hedge fund shorting the U.S. subprime mortgage market, but Joseph and Pharaoh acquiring grain when its value was low and selling much later when its value was high.

According to the Book of Genesis (41:1–57), Joseph interpreted Pharaoh's dream of seven fat cows followed by seven lean ones as a prediction for seven years of bountiful harvests followed by seven years of drought. Acting on inside information of the highest order, Joseph spent seven years collecting massive quantities of grain on behalf of Pharaoh. When the drought began and famine spread, Joseph sold and bartered the grain. Because the value of grain had shot up, these sales enabled Pharaoh to acquire all the money in Egypt and vastly expand his lands.

The story of Joseph and Pharaoh showed me what I was missing as I tried to make sense of investor behavior. Investment management involves more than information about which asset to buy or sell. To take a leap with other people's money and hold on for the long term, an investment manager must have a truly extraordinary ability to communicate her beliefs through a chain of actors and inspire those actors to maintain their resolve.

After interpreting Pharaoh's dream, Joseph went on to offer some unsolicited advice: hire a wise and discerning man (hint, hint) to oversee the grain-hoarding project. Why *wise and discerning?* Why not someone skilled at logistics or experienced with managing large enterprises? If everything Joseph predicted came true, the stockpile would grow for seven years with no drought in sight, testing the resolve of everyone in Egypt. After a few years, rival advisers, the military, priests, farmers, and perhaps Pharaoh himself might question the bet. Even Joseph might start to wonder whether the drought was really coming or worry that he had missed some hidden conditions. As the memory of prophecy dimmed, he might question whether he had misinterpreted the dream.

He did have a good track record, but track records come and go. In prison, he correctly predicted the fate of two other inmates: that Pharaoh's cupbearer would be restored to his position in three days while the baker would be hanged. That was out of the ordinary, for sure, but had he just gotten lucky? Had his luck now run out? At least one prophecy was yet to come true: Joseph's childhood dream that he would reign over his brothers.

Pressure must have mounted on Joseph to cut losses. Seven years is a long time to wait. Only a wise manager could maintain his nerve that long and inspire others to remain confident. Joseph and Pharaoh could not have fully transmitted the force of their belief to the people of Egypt, no matter how hard they tried. Their interior perspectives, molded by their experience, could not be shared. Verbal explanations would fail to communicate what prophecy is like. Instead, Joseph and Pharaoh relied on skill and authority to keep stakeholders at bay. Pharaoh not only hired Joseph but elevated him to a level seemingly unnecessary for an ordinary grain buyer. Upon appointing him, Pharaoh gave Joseph a signet ring, put a gold chain around his neck, clothed him in fine linen, and paraded him in front of the Egyptians in a chariot to show that Joseph was now his unequivocal number two. This authority allowed Joseph to accomplish his for-itself bet.

Joseph needed wisdom to hold onto his authority, which could have been snatched away at any moment. No matter how flexible the Egyptians may have been, it would have been impossible for Joseph and Pharaoh to convey their conviction; Joseph had a divine revelation and Pharaoh was there when it happened. This was unique. There were no words and certainly no mathematical models to describe the leap they had to take.

If my partners and I had the wisdom of Joseph or the authority of Pharaoh, no investor would have exited from our funds in 2008–2009 and we would have raised vast sums to buy at distressed prices. If we had inspired no confidence at all, everyone would have wanted to redeem from existing funds and we would have been unable to raise any fresh money. The reality was somewhere in between: about half of our investors redeemed, and new investments started to trickle into our funds in 2011.

From my point of view, investors who stayed on the sidelines in late 2008 through 2009 missed the chance to double or triple their money over two years without taking much risk. But I doubt any of them are kicking themselves now. As we've discussed, beliefs are inherently personal. So too, then, is a leap outside of them—an out-of-character act. Few institutional investors could take the sort of leap that bold bottom fishing required, no matter how hard the ardent believers tried to persuade them.

Years ago, I asked a well-known venture capitalist to give a short presentation to a class on economics and finance. The class had covered a fair amount of theory that I was hoping she would reinforce with colorful examples. We chatted ahead of time about what she might say, and she stayed on message right up to the end. But she closed her talk by saying that really, when she looks an entrepreneur in the eye, her gut tells her what to do. I could feel the students thinking, "Oh, I can do that." They wondered why they'd bothered with all the theory I'd been trying to teach them as a semester's progress melted away.

Since then, I've hardly ever invited guest speakers. But the venture capitalist was right, in a way. She is in the business of betting on hunches that can't be fully communicated. Her investors and limited partners get that. Every time she launches a new fund, her investors enter into a binding legal agreement to leave her alone for seven years—same as Joseph—to prove what she can do. It's the twenty-first-century signet ring.

PART III

People

Can't buy me love.

—JOHN LENNON AND PAUL MCCARTNEY

6

Altruism

The Good Samaritan's good deed in the biblical parable satisfies the definition of altruism: a voluntary action undertaken at cost to the actor to advance someone else's interests. The story begins with a man, beaten and robbed, lying half-dead on the road from Jerusalem to Jericho. Two men pass by without offering aid—indeed, without pausing to see whether he's alive or dead. But not the Samaritan. He stops, dresses the man's wounds, takes him to an inn, ministers to him, and as he's leaving, gives the innkeeper money to care for him. The Samaritan voluntarily incurred a cost of time and money for which he could not have expected a reward. It was an expression of concern for the welfare of a stranger. Does that make the behavior for-itself? Before jumping to that conclusion, let's take a look at the different categories of altruism.

Some prosocial dealings can easily be explained in terms of rational choice. At one end of the spectrum, other people are instrumental to our purposes. We work together to achieve common goals, engage in mutually beneficial activities, and perform favors in expectation of future favors. At the other end of the spectrum, our connection to others is so tight that their interests become our interests. The actions we take on their behalf have a purpose, and rational choice can explain how we optimize our desires alongside those we love or who love us. In the middle of the spectrum, however, we confront others as more than objects yet less than extensions of ourselves. Rather than purposeful, this category of altruism is spontaneous and for-itself.

A Taxonomy of Altruism

We can distinguish five main categories of altruistic behavior: (1) *selfish altruism*, when an individual appears to subordinate his interests while actually promoting them; (2) *manners and ethics*, when an individual observes social norms or adheres to established moral principles; (3) *care altruism*, when one person cares directly about the well-being of another; (4) *mercy*, when a person performs a sporadic altruistic act that defies rational explanation; and (5) *love altruism*, which describes acts that transcend all preferences and do not stand in relation to them. The purposeful choice model makes room for the first three types of altruism but not the last two.

Inherently Selfish Altruistic Behavior

Although "selfish" has a negative connotation, selfish altruism need not be sinister. It can be as innocent as doing a favor for a friend or business associate in anticipation of payback. (If the two parties have an explicit agreement, we wouldn't call it altruism—that's just doing business.) Selfish motives may be in play when people claim to be acting for the public good by volunteering, engaging in charity work, or donating money. If these activities are undertaken in order to appear generous, gain trust, or otherwise serve private interests, they are selfish.

The selfish altruist's most important tool is repeat dealing. It's widely known that if the prisoner's dilemma game is played only once, players seeking to maximize their payoff will choose the inefficient noncooperative solution. But if they play repeatedly and care about the present value of their payoff, they'll learn to cooperate. If one player cheats, the other will switch to the non-cooperative strategy, playing tit-for-tat until cooperation is restored. Each cooperative play, considered in isolation, looks selfless because either player could do better by cheating. But in the long run, cooperation leaves both better off.

In contexts like business, reputation can link all players together, even those who don't face off more than once. When each round is played with a new opponent, cooperative behavior can profit a self-interested person if subsequent opponents are aware of his reputation and have their own reputations to protect. Viewing each round in isolation, individuals once again appear altruistic, but under the surface each may be pursuing the optimal strategy for personal gain.[1]

Cynics may argue that all altruism is, at heart, selfish. This view can't be taken seriously. If, for example, private gain were the sole reason for volunteering, then everyone would know it was a ruse, it would fail to convey the intended message, and no one would do it. Recognizing that some altruism is selfish does not commit us to the depressing view that all altruism is.

Manners and Ethics

We may not consider polite behavior altruistic, but it meets our definition. Although instilled in us from an early age, manners can be understood as desires in the purposeful choice model and traded for a price. Adherence to basic social norms is predictable: I normally don't make phone calls on trains but will break that rule as a simple function of factors including the call's urgency and expected length, the number of people in the car I'd disturb, and the quality of reception. Adherence to norms is rewarded with personal satisfaction and social acceptance; the violation of norms incurs a cost.

Acting in accordance with an ethical code can also be understood as purposeful. While rules would dictate the same behavior each time the same circumstances arise, people sometimes act against their ethical codes, suggesting that these codes are not hard and fast rules. Rather, adherence to an ethical code is fundamentally a desire that must be balanced against other desires. This desire varies in intensity from person to person. When considering the right course of action, the depraved hardly care at all, the majority sometimes give way to expedience (placing a price on violating a principle, but a small one), and the most upright place a high price on rule breaking or reject expedience altogether.

If we accept that people prefer to abide by manners and principles when it doesn't cost them too much, we can interpret behavior in experiments like the "ultimatum game" as purposeful. This game is played by two anonymous people. The "allocator" proposes how to split a fixed pot, say ten dollars, between himself and the "receiver." The receiver can either accept or reject her share. If she accepts, she gets to keep it. If she rejects, neither the receiver nor the allocator gets anything. If both players in a single-round game care only about money and trust the rules, the allocator should propose $9.99 for himself and $0.01 for the receiver. The receiver should accept, since $0.01 is better than nothing.

In experiments, though, that's not usually what happens. The data show that most allocators in developed countries propose roughly even splits. In a carefully designed study, researchers found that splits cluster around 50/50 in Ljubljana and Pittsburgh and around 60/40 in favor of the allocator in Tokyo and Jerusalem. Low offers tended to be rejected in all four cities, suggesting that receivers trade financial gain for a chance to punish flagrant inequality.[2]

The cost of conforming to social norms in most of the ultimatum game literature is fairly low—a few dollars here or there. But an experiment conducted in poor villages in India with pots of up to 160 days' wages found that higher stakes lead to more lopsided splits in favor of the allocator and less frequent rejections: as the price (to the allocator) of fair play and (to the receiver) of punishing unfairness went up, players tended to prioritize wealth maximization.[3]

Care Altruism

Bona fide care for someone else's well-being results in utility functions that are, in economics jargon, "interlocking." If a child's well-being is a direct input into her parent's well-being, then the parent demonstrates what I'll call *care altruism*; she desires that the child be happy. This can, but does not necessarily, work in both directions. Parents may or may not care about their children, and children may or may not care about their parents.

Care altruism can be split into two categories. In *observed care altruism*, the income of the benevolent person (the one who cares) is sufficiently high and the care is sufficiently intense that action results. In *unobserved care*, the benevolent person cares but not enough to incur a cost to do anything about it.

OBSERVED CARE ALTRUISM

Gary Becker's elegant Rotten Kid Theorem shows how one benevolent family member can theoretically cement a household into a single optimizing unit. In his model, the family acts as if it shared one utility function and one budget even if the children are "rotten," that is, concerned exclusively with their own consumption. They instinctively advance their own interests by maximizing household wealth so that the benevolent family member feels richer and obtains more of everything, including consumption for her children, rotten or not.[4]

The redistribution of wealth within the household arises automatically out of the preferences of the benevolent family member. (For the sake of simplicity, let's follow Becker and designate the mother as that family member.) The mother is not motivated by a desire to affirm her self-image as nurturing; nor is she concerned about equity or justice. She simply wants the children to be happy because their satisfaction enters directly into her own. In this setup, redistribution is never used as a form of discipline, since punishment would impose a deadweight loss on the family that everyone would have to absorb.

The Rotten Kid Theorem presents, at best, an idealized version of reality. It relies on the assumption that every member of the household has perfect information about how much everyone else values each outcome. It also assumes that one benevolent family member feels strongly enough to transfer some positive amount to all others. Given these assumptions, it would appear that every member of the household was altruistic and dedicated to maximizing collective welfare. In fact, the mother's behavior is care altruism and the rotten kid's is a special kind of selfish altruism. But since both act in the other's interest, bound by the mother's desire to maximize a common objective, an outsider wouldn't be able to detect the difference. Although the mother and the woman saving her drowning husband who we encountered in Chapter 1 both care deeply about their families, they are opposites for our purposes. The woman saving her husband is acting outside of a purposeful calculation, while the mother can be modeled in terms of her preferences.

The Rotten Kid Theorem involves observed care for a limited number of people. Another type of observed care, *effective altruism*, encompasses multitudes. It stems from concern over the well-being of everyone in the world, often including animals. The Australian philosopher Peter Singer, a prominent advocate of effective altruism, abides by the principle that people who live in rich countries are morally obligated to support charities that aid the global poor. He equates spending on luxuries when some people are starving to letting a child drown because you don't want to muddy your clothes.[5]

Effective altruists don't give more to people geographically close to them than to those far away. Nor do they spread their philanthropy around; instead they concentrate on charities they believe will have the greatest impact. Rather than giving when they feel a personal connection—to the university they attended, research on the disease that killed a friend, or a fundraiser to buy a new fire truck for their town—they support the organizations that most efficiently improve the welfare of those most in need.

They rarely volunteer for worthy causes, preferring to work long hours at the highest-paying job to maximize the amount they can donate.

You don't have to give away all or most of your money to be an effective altruist. Using the standard purposeful choice calculation, you give until the marginal benefit you derive from helping others equals the marginal cost of reducing your consumption. Effective altruists don't give enough to reduce suffering in the world by a material amount—that is, to the point where each marginal dollar they give becomes less effective.

But giving does increase the marginal benefit of their own consumption. To reduce spending on themselves, they first cut out the most superfluous expenses. For instance, they might break the habit of buying a four-dollar cup of coffee and instead spend fifty cents to make coffee at home. Once they've made all the easy sacrifices, subsequent cuts become increasingly painful. To save another fifty cents per day, they might have to cut out coffee altogether. Eventually, they reach the point where the satisfaction from the last dollar directed to their own consumption equals the marginal value they attribute to one more dollar donated to the poor. The largesse required for effective altruism of course depends on wealth and preferences. The test is whether a person gives enough to significantly affect her lifestyle and whether she gives to the causes she judges to be most beneficial to humankind.

Then there are *extreme* effective altruists. Like their plain vanilla counterparts, extreme effective altruists give where they believe they can do the most good. But extreme altruists feel extraordinarily deep bonds with everyone in the world and give until the extra cost in foregone satisfaction from a dollar spent on themselves equals its perceived benefit to a needy person. In contrast with ordinary effective altruists, they put themselves on equal footing with the rest of humanity, asking, "Do I need this more than a faraway stranger?" The significant income transfer required makes extreme effective altruism very rare. It's an exceptional person whose well-being depends so intensely on the well-being of strangers.[6]

UNOBSERVED CARE

To become observable, care altruism must involve strongly felt bonds. But care can, and often does, exist at levels too low to catalyze action. Someone who cares but not enough to act exemplifies what I'll call *"unobserved* care." Care, too faint to be observed, is everywhere. In 1759, Adam Smith wrote that even "the greatest ruffian, the most hardened violator of the laws of society, is not altogether without . . . principles in his nature, which interest him in the fortune of others."[7] The ruffian's care for others is weak. It's not a "concern," just an "interest." He doesn't quite possess principles—rather, he's "not altogether without" them. While his interest is real, he doesn't act on it.

People who desire private jets or the well-being of refugees may not spend money in these areas because their desire is too low and the price too high. For instance, I am a fan of the New York Yankees baseball team, a bond I share with my fellow fans, most of whom I've never met. The Yankees' standings enters into my preference rankings. But the impact of the Yankees' standings on my satisfaction is far too low for me to send them any positive amount of money so they can afford better players. I care—I just don't care enough. That doesn't make me a hypocrite. Care can be genuine even when it doesn't result in action.[8]

A thought experiment could be used to verify unobserved care: would you give up a small amount to provide a large benefit to others, assuming that no one would ever know that you were the source? If my donation could draw in millions so that the Yankees could acquire an All-Star pitcher, I might anonymously give one dollar. Thus the team's welfare must be part of my utility.[9]

Altruism fits into purposeful choice in all the examples discussed so far. In the case of selfish altruism, the connection to others is so tenuous that they become part of an optimization strategy to gratify the altruist's desires. Our motives to act in harmony with good manners, social norms, and ethical precepts can be evaluated relative to each other and to other desires. Care altruism can be observed when the altruist's connection to others is so tight that their well-being factors into her routine optimization strategy. It is unobservable when care is sincere but of a lower magnitude—when it is optimal to refrain from acting because other options are preferable. None of these cases presents a problem within purposeful choice.

Mercy

Nearly five hundred years ago, Montaigne observed: "There is a certain satisfaction which tickles me when I do a just action and make others content."[10] Researchers have rediscovered this tickle, dubbed it the "warm glow effect" and attempted to fold it into purposeful choice.[11] But because the pursuit of Montaigne's tickle involves a free exercise of will and prioritizes the *act* of helping over ensuring the optimal outcome, it is for-itself.

An act of for-itself, out-of-character altruism, or *mercy*, occurs in the Buddhist parable of two monks walking along a river. When they see a young woman struggling to cross, the senior monk picks her up and carries her to the other side. Later, the still-astonished junior monk asks his colleague why he did it, since the monks are not allowed contact with women. The senior monk replies that he carried the woman only briefly and asks why the junior monk is still carrying her in his mind.

This act belongs to a single, unique moment in time, in which the senior monk makes a decision outside the dictates of any universal rule. He doesn't set out to do a good deed—he responds to circumstances that arise in the natural course of his travels. Here, as in all for-itself acts, authenticity plays an important role. We might help a little old lady across the street when we encounter one, but we don't actively seek little old ladies in order to reduce the stock of unassisted street-crossings. We only undertake altruistic acts of this kind from time to time. Since the decision to help is an act of will, this behavior is by its nature sporadic and unpredictable.

These altruistic gestures are about the *act* of helping, rather than about finding the most efficient way to make the recipient better off. Assume the little old lady derives twenty cents from my help, it takes one minute to walk her across the street, and my after-tax wage is a dollar per minute. Even with perfect information about all these inputs, I would not be tempted to say: "Lady, you take sixty cents. I'm going to walk across the street more quickly by myself, and we'll both be forty cents better off." Nor would I hire someone on the street corner to walk her across for fifteen cents, even though that would leave me eighty-five cents better off than if I walked her across myself. I am not directly concerned about the little old lady's welfare—or at least, that's not what is driving me to help her.

A staunch defender of purposeful choice might argue that this gesture is care altruism: a burst of care for the old lady that lasts a moment, then disappears. But ephemeral priorities have no place in an optimization problem. A textbook condition for rational choice is reasonably stable preferences. If desires come and go willy-nilly, rational choice can no longer help explain our actions. Attributing them to random desires renders rational choice theory useless.

The defender of purposeful choice could instead try to cast

this act in terms of manners or ethics. Clearly, there is a contin-uum of cases. To take a more common example than the little old lady crossing the street, I, like many New Yorkers, volunteer every once in a while to assist tourists struggling with maps. I have no idea why I do this sometimes and not others. It defies any clear explanation and so is for-itself.

Love Altruism

Our taxonomy would be incomplete if it failed to encompass commitments that are greater than all preferences put together. This final for-itself category is embodied by the woman from Chapter 1 who jumps into the river to rescue her husband. The essential qualities of this act can't be captured by care altruism (or any other sort of purposeful altruism), or even mercy. My example has to do with love between people, but this category may also encompass the intensely religious who perform extraor-dinary deeds of renunciation out of love for God.

Some Examples of Acting with Mercy

"Mercy" describes an unpredictable, unselfish altruistic act that cannot be characterized by a direct preference for the well-being of another person. It can be effective or not, generous or not, and can coexist with other types of altruism. Risking one's own life in the spontaneous and heroic rescue of a stranger is clearly merciful. But even if helping the little old lady to cross the street is mundane and inefficient (it would be more efficient to give her sixty cents), it is still an act of spontaneous unselfishness since it delays my progress.

Unique acts of mercy for the good of a single individual and in defiance of cost-benefit calculations punctuate military campaigns. After U.S. Captain Roger Locher's plane crashed in Vietnam in 1972, General John Vogt "shut down the war" by sending 119 aircraft to rescue Locher. Vogt wasn't taking a page out of any strategy manual. As he later explained, it was a personal decision: "I took it on myself. I didn't ask anybody for permission."[12]

Merciful acts often fly in the face of the altruist's self-interest, as in the biblical story of Sodom and Gomorrah. When God shared with Abraham his plan to destroy the two cities, Abraham protested. God agreed to spare all of Sodom and Gomorrah if fifty righteous people could be found there. But Abraham kept bargaining: how about forty-five, forty, thirty, twenty? Finally, God agreed to call off the destruction if just ten righteous people could be found. (Even that was too tall an order: the next day, God leveled the cities with fire and brimstone.)

Sodom and Gomorrah were selfish societies that despised charity. They so opposed hospitality that the entire populace tried to punish angels lodging in Lot's house for relying on his hospitality rather than fending for themselves. Abraham's mission in life, according to the Jewish interpretation, was to promote kindness and charity. Abraham was no pacifist (just before this incident, he and his servants slaughtered the Elamites to rescue Lot), and getting Sodom and Gomorrah out of the way would certainly have made the world kinder and more charitable, but apparently, he didn't make that calculation. He didn't ask that only the righteous be saved, or for something better, like an end to famine. Instead, Abraham protested God's plan, squandering political capital out of mercy for all the cities' inhabitants, righteous or not.

The deep roots of our impulse toward occasional acts of mercy are evident in not only ancient religious texts but also the evolutionary heritage of primates, as Frans de Waal and his coauthors demonstrated in an experiment with female capuchin monkeys. Two monkeys were placed in adjoining cages. The "subject monkey" was then offered a choice between two tokens: (1) a "selfish" token that would result in a reward of fruit to only the subject monkey, or (2) a "prosocial" token that would result in the same reward to the subject monkey and an equal reward to the "partner monkey." The subject monkeys had the same role throughout the experiment, so there was no obvious potential for reciprocity.

The monkeys chose the prosocial token significantly more often than the selfish token, especially as the experiment progressed and they learned what the tokens meant. The monkeys were also more likely to choose the prosocial token if their partners were visible to them or belonged to the same social group.[13] This fits with Montaigne's tickle theory: it's more pleasing when you can see your altruism in action and when you know the recipient. But the monkeys didn't choose the prosocial token every time. Perhaps they wanted each act to be their idea, when the spirit moved them.

A variation on this experiment demonstrated that the monkeys did not care directly about the *welfare* of their partners. Rewards for the prosocial token were made unequal, so that the subject monkey received a piece of apple while the partner received a grape, which capuchin monkeys prefer. This should have made subject monkeys who cared directly about their partner's welfare even more likely to choose the prosocial token, since the greater reward to the partner came at no cost to them. But when the prosocial token came with a larger reward for the partner, the subject monkeys ceased to prefer it. They enjoyed a good deed, but only up to a point.[14]

While such studies establish an ingrained tendency toward mercy, each act of mercy is unique. If we were merciful all the time, then we would no longer be acting out of mercy but adhering to rules.

Still, a scheduled charitable act could be merciful if it preserved an element of spontaneity. Suppose someone decided to donate money each week but left the implementation to whimsy. This week, give it all to a charity for seeing-eye dogs; next week, split it between the opera and the Red Cross; and so forth. This feels mostly purposeful—to the extent the acts are planned, they become expressions of ethical principles—but also retains a for-itself element.

Sometimes it's hard to untangle the purposeful from the for-itself. The first time we watch *Casablanca*, we are moved when Rick sends Ilsa on the plane with her husband to freedom. Rick implies that he wrestled with it the night before, but the viewer gets the impression he's making the final decision then and there. That would make it a for-itself gesture of mercy, but there must also be at least a little truth in his famous claim that Ilsa would eventually regret leaving her husband. That suggests a hint of care altruism and maybe selfish concern that her unhappiness would trickle down to him.

A One-Time Act of Mercy

We all engage in mundane acts of mercy from time to time. Around five years ago, I put aside a rule that organizes my life in favor of such an act. Even after all this time, my decision still puzzles me.

For my lecture classes, I have a no-nonsense approach to grading. Each student's grade index is 45 percent her midterm exam score, 45 percent her final exam score, and 10 percent her homework scores. The exams are mostly multiple choice, and short answers are graded according to transparent rules. The grade indices are rigidly mapped onto letter grades around a mean of B+.

As soon as grades are posted, I receive a barrage of protest emails. After checking to make sure the disgruntled student's final exam was properly marked, I send a standard response:

Dear Mr./Ms. X,
The grades are determined according to a formula. Here are
your inputs . . . The formula produces a numerical index that
maps onto letter grades according to the following grid . . . It is
the same for everyone. I do hope you learned useful things in
the class that will serve you after grades have been forgotten.

If the student's index comes just below a threshold, I add:

Your grade was nearly an A– but unfortunately did not make
the cutoff. That's bad luck. I hope that over the course of your
life, good luck will eclipse the bad.

Usually they accept my response and that's the end of it. Occasionally, a student who has apparently read a book about "Getting to Yes" asks: "What can I do to improve my grade?" My answer is always: "I can't offer an option to you unless I also offer it to everyone else." If the student still doesn't give up, I write: "The only way is to invent a time machine, go back in the past, and study harder."

Once, I received an email from a student who said she was in jeopardy of losing her Singaporean government sponsorship as a result of her B– grade. I didn't know this student and barely recognized her name, meaning she wasn't an active participant in class and hadn't come by for help during office hours. Grades in my classes are a function of effort, so I felt confident that the B– was her fault.

But just as I was about to send the usual it's-the-same-for-everyone email, I switched her grade to a B. I asked her not to tell anyone, and as far as I know she didn't.

Why did I give her a break? I had nothing to gain. I'd never see her again and didn't care about her personally because I didn't know her. Nor could I justify it in terms of some moral precept to act for the common good. Presumably, if this young woman lost her fellowship, the money would go to a student more deserving of Singapore's assistance, one who legitimately earned the required grades.

In terms of identifiable interests, however, I did have something to lose. If word got out that I was arbitrarily changing grades, this one act of mercy would have opened the floodgates to similar petitions. For obvious reasons, I didn't want to set myself up as the judge of each student's circumstances. It could have become a slippery slope, quickly reducing my grading process from order to chaos. Now that five years have passed, I can safely say that I didn't slip down that slope: I've never bestowed a similar act of mercy on another student.

Given that I had no incentive to favor her plea over all the others and good reasons to dismiss it, did I behave irrationally? Was I losing my grip? I don't think so, even though this act of altruism can't be explained by purposeful choice. It was a spontaneous, random, one-time gesture of mercy. I am not proud of helping her, nor do I regret it. I can only say that I did it. It was out of character and for-itself and cannot be explained by an appeal to any motive beyond acting with mercy.

Love Altruism Redux

Let's revisit the woman from the beginning of this book who jumps into the river to save her drowning husband. We'll add some details to their story.

The husband hardly ever walks their dog because the wife bought it and he never wanted it in the first place. Sometimes the wife has to leave her office early to walk the dog, even though the husband is already home. Left to himself, he doesn't mind getting a little exercise, but he won't walk the dog because he sees it as his wife's responsibility.

When the wife returns home, she scolds her husband for his selfishness. Scolding is unpleasant for him, but he doesn't change his behavior. The wife likes venting, but not as much as her husband dislikes being on the receiving end.

This suggests that the two don't care about each other in the sense that the wife's well-being enters into her husband's utility or vice versa. Of course, if the dog were the only contentious issue, we could overlook it. But to prove there is one more category of for-itself altruism, let's continue with our example. Let's assume there are many such cases where one spouse fails to expend a minor effort that would deliver a larger benefit to the other. This is not to say they have a bad marriage—they just don't attribute value to each other's well-being. They may regularly help each other, exemplifying two varieties of purposeful altruism: selfish altruism (that is, trading favors) and social norms. They may enjoy each other's company and mean it when they say that their marriage is a happy one. But they don't *care* directly about each other's well-being.[15]

Nonetheless, the wife can love her husband. To be precise: when he's drowning in the river, she suspends the entire schema that defines her purposeful actions. In this instance, love is not a desire and saving her beloved is not a preference. The commitment to her many preferences is no greater than her love of her husband. It's not mercy; she might jump into the river every time the same situation arises. But she can't supply a reason that would mean much. A reason for jumping would be in reference to her other choices, and this one doesn't fit. Its authority is bigger than any means, ends, or trade-offs.

It would be wrong to try to cast the woman's choice as unobserved care that rises to the surface when the husband's life is in danger. To make the point logically, we can embellish the example further by supposing that as soon as her husband is out of the river, the wife resumes her nagging. Or we can provide for other conduct that substantially diminishes her husband's quality of life. Still, when the time comes, she jumps.

We've mentioned a few extraordinary for-itself acts of mercy, for example, the senior monk who carries the woman and the saving of Captain Locher, but those are logically different from love altruism. They are sporadic, whereas the woman might try to save her husband every time. Nor are those acts of mercy driven by strong bonds with the recipient. Most importantly, we don't have to say that the senior monk and the American general were drawn to these acts by forces greater than all their other concerns. I am not denying that there are borderline cases—perhaps the end of *Casablanca*—where we could argue for mercy or love altruism. But either way, it's for-itself.

Malevolence

Selfish altruism has a counterpart in strategic competition. In a game of chess, we're happy to lose a piece as long as our opponent loses one of greater value. This behavior is clearly purposeful. But just as a self-interested performance of favors lacks the goodwill associated with altruism, strategic competition lacks the vindictiveness and smoldering ill will that evoke acts of malevolence.

Strategic competition aside, modeling malevolence isn't as simple as applying our taxonomy of prosocial altruism in reverse. Consider the manners or ethical code branch: while some societies care a great deal about vengeance, most moral codes stress loving your neighbor rather than harming your enemy.

Nor is there a clear analog for the observed care altruism modeled with the Rotten Kid Theorem. People rarely expend resources up to the point where they equate the loss to themselves to the loss to their enemy. A struggle so bitter that one person hates another as passionately as a mother loves her child is inherently unstable. Very soon, the malevolent person would destroy her enemy. Even unobserved care malevolence, caring about my enemy's distress enough to trade my own distress for it at some ratio, seems implausible. Suppose I was walking down an isolated street and came across my enemy's parked car. It would only take a moment to throw a rock through his windshield and no one would ever suspect that I was the culprit. Yet I can't conceive of doing something so deranged.

And finally, the reverse of effective altruism would be monstrous: except in cases of mental illness, no one has a general desire to harm strangers. A disturbed person who feels wronged by life may enjoy inflicting pain from time to time, but to qualify as a reverse effective altruist, she would have to devote herself to inflicting the maximum possible pain on humanity as a whole. While a terrorist might want to wreak damage on a particular population, he acts out of selfish malevolence to achieve a political agenda, albeit mixed with pleasure from harming his enemies.

Love altruism has a straightforward malevolent counterpart in crimes of passion. There must also be a malevolent counterpart to mercy, since neither the pleasures of malevolence nor the sweetness of revenge can be denied. In for-itself malevolence—let's call it *spite*—it's the act that matters. The opportunity for this type of malevolence must arise in a natural context, and the punishment ideally preys on the enemy's flaws. Poetic justice is sweet in real life as well as in fiction.

One of literature's most artful acts of vengeance occurs in Edgar Allan Poe's "The Cask of Amontillado." After a chance encounter during a carnival, Montresor exploits his enemy Fortunato's vanity to lure him to his doom in the catacombs. This murder is premeditated—Montresor has simply been waiting for the right opportunity. Spontaneity plays a less crucial role in spite than in mercy, since the most inventive punishments often require a degree of planning. And while mercy can benefit a stranger, spite involves strong animosity toward a particular individual. As in all well-constructed malevolent acts, the victim here recognizes the author of his downfall.

There are a few other key differences between mercy and spite. While we can only pursue a small fraction of the abundant chances that life affords us to act altruistically, opportunities to enjoy the pleasures of spite are rare. (Given that the malevolent act need only seem artful to the actor, people with low standards might find more opportunities for for-itself malevolence.) And despite philosopher Jeremy Bentham's claim that malevolence is one of life's basic pleasures, it may come with inner conflict.[16] Acts of malevolence, especially ones that violate our ethical principles, can generate nagging feelings of guilt and self-doubt. Fifty years later, Montresor was still rationalizing his crime.

Regret versus Remorse

Regret and remorse are different classes of feeling, but if we view all behavior as purposeful, we risk confusing them.

The anodyne case of regret occurs when we make an error while attempting to optimize. When people say they feel regret, they might simply mean that with hindsight, they recognize that they would be better off had they chosen differently. Or maybe they mean that they miscalculated: if they had thought more carefully, they would have acted differently. Regret belongs squarely in the purposeful realm. We should be able to learn from mistakes and let regret fade into the past.

Remorse is not simply a stronger version of regret—it belongs to a different category. It would be unremarkable to say that I feel *regret* for not buying gold in 1986, since its price increased by a factor of three over the next thirty-three years. It would sound strange, however, to say that I feel *remorse* for not buying Microsoft stock at its 1986 initial public offering, even though it increased by a factor of five hundred over the same period. I just feel more regret about Microsoft stock than I do about gold.

If a person makes a profound error in judgment or commits an immoral act, the remedy (if there is one) is to repent. That repentance, like the original act, stands for itself. Repentance can't be outsourced. Scapegoats, sin eaters, and the buying of indulgences have all passed into history. Charitable giving (which is not exempt from purposeful calculations) may help relieve a general sense of guilt, but it cannot assuage remorse over a particular act. If that act was not part of an optimization problem, then the subsequent contrition cannot be either.

Jean-Paul Sartre tells the story of a student whose brother was killed in the war in 1940. The student is torn: he feels compelled to join the Free French Forces but also to stay at home and care for his mother, who would suffer without him.[17] This is more than just a difficult decision. He can weigh the chance that he would affect the outcome of the war against the likely impact of his absence on his mother, and either way, he could argue afterward that he chose wisely within the context of his moral precepts. Nonetheless, his decision cannot possibly be cast in the framework of purposeful choice. He can't quantify and compare the benefits of fighting against the costs of abandoning his mother—he's grappling with love altruism for his mother, his country, and his brother's memory, rendering the decision for-itself. Whatever he chooses, he is destined to feel remorse. But that does not mean he'll necessarily feel regret; he can simultaneously feel remorse over his decision and believe it was the right one. If he could do it over, he'd make the same choice.

Back to the Good Samaritan

The Good Samaritan did nothing noteworthy by stopping to check on the beaten man. That could have been predicted: it's likely he would have stopped every time he found himself in a similar situation. He was merely exercising the values instilled by his upbringing. Since adherence to principles or social mores is purposeful, we can model his response with rational choice.

But taking the beaten man to the inn, caring for him, and paying the innkeeper to continue caring for him lifts the Samaritan's behavior into a different category. If he'd lavished that degree of attention on every needy person he met, he'd never have made his way out of Jerusalem. This altruism was unpredictable and so qualifies as for-itself mercy.

As we've discussed, several or all five categories of altruism can be in play at the same time. The Samaritan could have gone the extra mile partly out of selfish altruism if he planned to bolster his reputation by telling the story afterward. Or maybe he was an extreme effective altruist and felt deeply about the welfare of the beaten man and everyone else besides. But none of this explains the extravagance of his gesture, all the time and money spent on one person.

7

Public Policy

I've presented the argument that much of altruistic behavior is purposeful, and some is for-itself. In light of this distinction, let's look at policies adopted by individuals and particularly by governments to advance collective welfare. Many policies rely in straightforward ways on purposeful choice economics. (We'll use the term "purposeful" here rather than "rational" to allow for policies that exploit behavioral biases.) These policies can be boiled down to a fixed set of rules that maximize a well-defined concept of the public good. But other policy problems cannot be solved by even the most sophisticated application of purposeful choice and instead require tough, for-itself decisions. This discussion will not resolve intractable policy problems or moral dilemmas, but we can gain insight by assigning them to their proper realms.

Pareto Efficiency and Purposeful Public Policy

One simple rule, *Pareto efficiency*, can be used to determine whether a policy can be evaluated in terms of purposeful choice. In purposeful choice, one policy is superior to another if and only if it is Pareto efficient, that is, the superior policy helps someone and hurts no one, or at least makes the winners better off by a sufficiently large margin that they could theoretically compensate the losers and no one would be worse off. This approach assumes that policymakers can determine the preferences of all their constituents, including their constituents' ethical principles and the weight given to those principles. It's not practical, but that's a technical issue which doesn't affect whether a policy problem is purposeful or for-itself.[1]

Suppose a factory emits pollution that imposes health costs of $1 million on people who live nearby. It would be Pareto efficient to force the factory to pay $300,000 to install equipment that would reduce the impact of the pollution to $100,000. The factory owner would then be $300,000 worse off, but if those who most benefited from the reduced pollution chipped in to compensate him, everyone would win. If profits before installing the equipment were less than $300,000, another Pareto improvement could be achieved by shutting down the factory.

To measure the health costs ($1 million in this example), we'd estimate the total amount that each person afflicted would be willing to pay to reduce the factory's pollution to zero, assuming everyone had perfect information. An even better estimate would tack on social costs, such as health care paid by the government.

Some decisions, however, must be made without the guidance of Pareto efficiency. Political scientist Michael Taylor provides an example in the story of Arizona's Yavapai Indians, who would refuse "all the money in the world" from a federal bureau intent on building a dam on their ancestral lands.[2] They could not be adequately compensated by any material good for the loss of what they have. It simply might not be possible to relocate the native people, give them a monetary side payment, and make everyone better off. Society, in deciding whether to let the government build a dam, would have to make a for-itself decision about whether the benefit of the electricity exceeds its costs to an unwilling few.

Two Moral Dilemmas

The distinction between purposeful and for-itself decision-making can be demonstrated by looking at two enduring moral puzzles: the merchant's choice posed by Cicero in 44 BCE and the trolley problem posed by Philippa Foot in 1967.[3] The merchant's choice belongs in the purposeful category, where options can be evaluated, ranked, and traded. Choices in the trolley problem, however, depend ultimately on impulse—attempts to calculate the trade-offs are swamped by an individual exercise of will. Action (or inaction) is for-itself.

In Cicero's story, Rhodes is suffering a famine when a merchant arrives at the port with a ship full of grain. The merchant knows that other ships carrying grain are en route. If, as Cicero tells us, the merchant is virtuous, must he inform the starving buyers that further supply is on the way, thereby reducing the price he can charge? Two cynics, Antipater and Diogenes, debate the matter.

Antipater and Diogenes agree that disclosure would be nice, all else being equal. But Diogenes argues that the merchant is not obligated to reveal this information because there is a significant difference between not revealing and actively concealing. Antipater favors disclosure on the basis that "it is your duty to consider the interests of your fellow-men and to serve society."[4]

The primary impact of disclosure would be on the market-clearing price and hence on the merchant's profit. Either way, the people of Rhodes, taken as a whole, will end up with the same amount of grain on the same schedule.[5] Thus the question is really, how much money should the Rhodians transfer to the merchant? And how important is the principle that honesty is the best policy? Omitting material facts is not as bad as lying, but it still wouldn't be the merchant's finest moment. The merchant must consider how his actions will affect his reputation if he plans to do business in Rhodes again or if word of his conduct spreads beyond Rhodes. He'll necessarily evaluate all these factors in the context of his wealth—if he's struggling, he'll tilt the scales in favor of not disclosing. None of the values in play are absolute.

The merchant can weigh the social and personal implications of this decision, then decide whether the potential collective gains from disclosing outweigh the private benefits of keeping quiet. Likewise, Antipater and Diogenes can deliberate, hone their views, and factor in self-interest. Still, their behavior is predictable: Antipater would always favor disclosing. Diogenes would be less inclined to disclose unless the damage from concealing was very great. Every aspect of this debate fits into the purposeful choice framework. It's possible to do the necessary calculations to rationally balance concern for public welfare, private gain, and ethical principles.

At the opposite extreme from the merchant's choice is the trolley problem. There are many versions of the thought experiment originally posed by Philippa Foot; in one of the most famous, five people are standing on trolley tracks with a runaway trolley car hurtling toward them. You are standing on a bridge over the tracks next to a fat man. Pushing him onto the tracks would kill him but stop the trolley and save five people.[6]

What might drive you to do it? Not selfish altruism, since you have nothing to gain (and in fact something to lose: you could be charged with manslaughter). Not care altruism, unless you're an effective altruist, because you have no connection to any of the potential victims. It's possible that personal moral principles would dictate a particular response—a utilitarian might favor pushing, while a Kantian might not. For effective altruists, utilitarians, and Kantians, the moral considerations arising from the trolley problem fit with purposeful choice. As long as they don't abandon their principles at the crucial moment, their actions should be predictable. For the rest of us, though, it might not be so easy.

The trolley problem is carefully constructed so that there is no Pareto-efficient solution. Variations of the problem that deal with injury, where everyone can be made better off, are easy to solve. Say the man you pushed would break his arm to save five people from breaking their arms. Well, then go ahead and push, since you can make it up to him later. At least in principle, the five people who avoided injury could pay him part of their gain from not breaking their arms, leaving everyone better off. But if the fat man is a shot putter about to compete in the Olympics, don't push, since the cost of breaking his arm likely exceeds the sum cost of breaking the arms of five random people. In the actual trolley problem, though, he can't be compensated for blocking the trolley since he'll be dead.

I don't think we can resort to a "veil of ignorance" solution, either. If I didn't know ex ante whether I'd be the fat man or one of the five people on the tracks and I had a one-sixth chance of each, of course I would choose "push." But that doesn't help with the trolley problem. It is already resolved who will be the fat man and that's the individual you'd have to kill.

In the end, I probably wouldn't push, although I can't say for sure. It would depend on the details. Like many people, I'd be more likely to push if the fat man were a villain, if children were

on the tracks, or if the number of potential victims were significantly greater than five. But even though I probably wouldn't
push, I won't argue that others should make the same choice. It's
a for-itself act: no moral principle that I hold would fully justify
favoring one life over five, and no amount of calculation would
simplify the problem.

If you favored pushing, I wouldn't quarrel. We'd just have to
disagree, although "disagree" is the wrong word, since I couldn't
make a rational case for my decision. In a sense, I'd probably
prefer that you push, since the lives of five abstract people matter more to me than one. But "prefer" isn't quite right, either—
let's just say that I guess I'd be pleased if I learned after the fact
that you had pushed. I'm not going to encourage you to do it,
though—that's too close to pushing myself.

What would Antipater and Diogenes have to say about the
trolley problem? They could talk all day, debating ethical rules
and practical consequences. But while they might convince me
to take one side or the other in the merchant's problem, they
almost certainly couldn't convince me that there's a correct solution to the trolley problem.

My point is not to sermonize on which actions are right or
wrong, but rather to consider how we *do* behave when actions
have moral dimensions. In some cases, we weigh moral principles: it's wrong to withhold information, worse to lie. Violating
these principles would impose costs to varying degrees on the
merchant. At the same time, he seeks to earn a profit. All these

factors contribute to his decision. Since he is acting purposefully, we should expect a reasonably consistent response when similar problems arise in the future. He might disclose sometimes and not others, but that doesn't necessarily make him inconsistent, since the particulars might differ. A for-itself component might also influence his decision if he's moved by an impulse to aid the Rhodians.

In other cases, there's little weighting to be done and little self-interest to consider, and valid principles conflict with each other: it's wrong to cause one person to be killed and also wrong to allow five people to be killed. Since most of us lack a unifying system that dictates which principle should trump the others, the problem is fundamentally for-itself.

Computing the Monetary Value of a Life

If the trolley problem were posed to you, you might refuse to answer. You could say, "I don't know. It would depend on countless particulars, and I don't know myself well enough to answer with confidence. Maybe I would push sometimes but not others. The act is unpredictable and for-itself."

That's a perfectly fine answer for an individual confronted with hypotheticals, but in the arena of public policy, society cannot avoid addressing real-world analogs to the trolley problem. Whom should we save when resources are limited? How much should we spend to save them? Should we raise the speed limit to reduce the travel time of five million people by ten minutes each at the cost of one extra traffic death? Here, rational choice provides the only sensible guidance.

Government policies involving everything from the military to health and safety have a direct bearing on life and death. Callous though it may seem, the cost-benefit analysis for these decisions necessarily attaches numbers to life. The standard approach estimates the expected present value of someone's lifetime earnings plus the monetary value of the services she provides to her family, such as emotional comfort. Another approach infers the value that people place on their own lives from the risks that they take. According to this calculation, someone willing to pay up to but no more than $100 for safety equipment that would reduce his risk of death by 0.001 percent values his life at around $10 million.

This type of calculus shapes auto safety regulation. The government directs labor and capital to make safer cars, but only up to a point. It determines speed limits in a similar way. Lowering the highway speed limit to twenty miles per hour would sharply reduce traffic fatalities, but most everyone would object to frittering away more time sitting in cars. Transportation departments must balance time wasted against the value of the expected extra lives lost when raising the speed limit.

We can cast this argument in terms of Pareto efficiency. People vary with respect to the cost they assign to driving very slowly and the value they implicitly assign to their lives. Suppose a policy raising the speed limit to 70 mph has been proposed, and a few people who are rarely in a hurry and care a great deal about safety object. These cautious people could, in principle, be compensated from a tax on those who benefit from the higher speed limit, leaving everyone better off. The fact that it's hard to identify the winners and losers from this policy and impractical to implement the transfer doesn't invalidate the calculation.

It's a losing argument to maintain that assigning a finite monetary value to human life crosses a moral line. Government officials must make calculated choices. No one can know who will die in traffic accidents, so policymakers are unlikely to feel a connection to future victims. This allows them to maintain the level of abstraction that the calculation requires. Even if the official in charge of speed limits refuses to explicitly assign a value to human life, she still does so implicitly.

The value-of-a-life calculation becomes more difficult for a congress or head of state declaring war, and more difficult still for a military officer sending specific individuals into battle. The general will likely feel a mix of emotions over purposefully calculating the value of the lives of people he knows. Generals like Alexander the Great have mitigated this unease by personally leading troops into battle, communicating that they value the soldiers' lives on the same scale as their own.

Every day, in dozens of ways, modern, unadventurous civilians implicitly assign value to lives—their own, the lives of their families, and those of strangers. Someone asked how much money he would accept for his child's life would probably object that such a calculation was impossible and that the question was unthinkable. Yet the Department of Transportation official who assigns a value to a life and the parent who refuses to put a number on his child's life can coexist (in fact, they could be the same person). When it comes time to act, the parent makes calculations, too. When my son, Nathan, was an infant, I chose a larger, safer car than I would otherwise have bought. But I did not buy an armored car, which would have been more expensive and harder to park.

If you want to live in the world, then there's no way to completely avoid the abstraction necessary for purposeful calculations. But the necessity of making these calculations doesn't mean you must answer questions like "At what odds would you bet your child's life for a dollar?" in order to be rational. First, the question is spiritually degrading to entertain. Second, even if you answered 1:1 trillion, how could you trust the questioner not to cheat? After all, he's prepared to kill your children if he wins. The odds that you've misunderstood the rules or misjudged the laws of the universe may exceed the likelihood of a very unlucky outcome from a conventional random number generator.

The philosopher John Searle poses this question in terms of a paradox. On the one hand, he objects strenuously to the idea that he should be willing to bet his life for twenty-five cents if the odds are sufficiently high. He considers the wager absurd and can't conceive of a probability close enough to one. Even if he could, he says, he would not wager, at any odds, his child's life or the survival of humankind for a quarter.[7]

On the other hand, Searle concedes that he willingly takes many small risks of death in exchange for a benefit, sometimes even a monetary benefit. For example, he would agree to drive someone to the San Francisco airport for $1,000, even though his risk of death would be lower if he stayed home. But if he thinks of the trip as four thousand equally sized increments, isn't he effectively taking one four-thousandth of the risk over each increment in exchange for a quarter?[8]

Driving someone to the airport arises naturally in life, so we are likely to have confidence in the rules of the game. We have less confidence in theoretical scenarios. Who is this homicidal genie who asks me to bet my life against a quarter? Does he have the intent and ability to carry out the murder if I lose? How do I know the rules are as he describes them? Maybe it's a trick. I don't have any experience with supernatural beings who pose these kinds of questions—who knows what they have up their sleeves? I might propose a-trillion-to-one odds for my life versus a quarter, but how do I account for the odds that the genie is cheating?

Driving your child somewhere or, for that matter, allowing her to leave the house, indicates a willingness to tolerate some amount of risk for some benefit. But fortunately for you, unless you are a policymaker dealing with such questions, you don't have to assign an abstract value to life. You can reject the question because it mixes the purposeful (money) with the for-itself (your child's life)—two things that cannot be compared.

PART IV

Time

In "economic" life . . . the motivation of competitive sport plays a role at least as great as the endeavor to secure gratifications mechanically dependent on quantitative consumption . . . The real problem centers, of course, in the fact that activity has both characters; it is a game, but one in which the most vital substantive goods, comfort and life itself, are stakes, inseparably combined with victory and defeat and their bauble-symbols.

—Frank Knight, "The Role of Principles in Economics and Politics"

8

Changing Our Minds

Suppose you buy an expensive motorcycle to get around town, but it's not quite as much fun as you expected. You return it and buy a small car for the same price. But you find the car hard to park and miss the motorcycle. You return the car, buy the same motorcycle, and keep it. You may feel a little foolish, but this is hardly cause for alarm as long as you don't do it too often. Your preferences for transportation, safety, and fun never budged—you just learned a few things through experience. This is rational choice at work.

Now, suppose a middle-aged man buys a motorcycle rather than a car out of nostalgia for his happy, carefree, younger days riding on the Pacific Coast Highway. But the motorcycle doesn't fit his suburban lifestyle. He quickly sells it back to the dealer and buys a car. His mistake was allowing emotionally charged memories, rather than rational deliberation, to guide his decision. He acted on a behavioral bias and, one hopes, will learn from his mistake.

In both of these examples, ending up with the right vehicle required learning of some kind. But suppose that you know perfectly what your desires are and how to satisfy them. There are no surprises in your world, and you have all the information you need without learning from experience. You buy a new motorcycle, and it's everything you dreamed it would be. You never tire of riding it. Yet you still have difficult decisions to make. You lead a busy life, and riding cuts into your work and hence your earnings. How often and when do you indulge in your new favorite pastime? Even as a well-informed and rational actor, is it still possible that you'd change your mind over time?

Imagine that a demon shows up and demands that you pick a motorcycle riding plan, once and for all, for all future days. The demon makes you choose for yourself and enforces whatever you select. You consider every possible plan available to you—a constant amount of working at your job and riding every day; working like a madman for years and riding for days on end later; or living for the moment, riding today and working hard tomorrow. You rank all the options and choose the one you like the best.

In this context, changing your mind would mean wanting to break from the plan you agreed to. For example, when the demon first arrived, it may have seemed like a good idea that today should be dedicated to recreation and tomorrow to austerity. But once tomorrow arrives, austerity no longer feels like the way to go. If the demon would let you off, you'd head back to the open road. (It's assumed in this thought experiment that you trust the demon when you make your choice the first time around. That is, you're not choosing with a view toward bargaining later on.)

Can this be rational? Is it possible for rational actors to change their minds even in the absence of new information, to want to get off the path they agreed to with the demon? Not only is it possible but, as we'll see shortly, it's inevitable. Eventually, even rational actors always change their minds.

In the real world, there is no demon to make you pick once and for all. If your idea on Monday about what to do on Tuesday no longer seems best when Tuesday rolls around, you can rethink it. Whether deciding how much to ride your motorcycle or how much money to spend, you can choose what you would like to do now, then choose again later. It wouldn't matter if one of your previous incarnations emerged from thin air to boss you around, saying, "I would have picked something different." That person is gone—you owe her nothing.

There are times, no doubt, when an enforcement demon would be helpful. In the absence of one, you might seek a *commitment device* to force your future self to do the bidding of today's self. The prototypical example of such a device comes from Homer's *Odyssey*. Odysseus wanted to hear the Sirens' song but knew it would compel him to leap from the ship to join them at his peril.

Before the ship reached earshot, he had the crew tie him tightly to the mast and plug their own ears with wax.

On a less heroic scale, I keep my alarm clock across the room from my bed to force myself to get up. Acting on similar logic, someone who drives to a party might immediately give his car keys to a teetotaling neighbor who can drive him home, anticipating that he'll be too inebriated later to make a sound decision.

But let's not make too much of these examples; the occasional need for a commitment device does not imply that some deep instability pervades everyday life. Odysseus, the alarm-setter, and the partygoer all know they will experience a nonrational state in the near future. Odysseus will fall under the Sirens' spell, the person setting the alarm clock will be groggy, and the partygoer will be drunk. Preparing for a temporary, anticipated loss of judgment is rational.

As long as we take steps to keep ourselves on track during periods of impaired judgment, changing our minds (deviating from the path we'd agree to with the demon) does not present a serious problem for individuals. It does, however, for economists attempting to model the way we save, consume, and invest. They will be disappointed by real people who do not and cannot trade present well-being for future well-being in some grand optimization problem.

When we depart from their models, frustrated economists might conclude that we suffer from a dysfunctional relationship with time. It may not occur to them that we simply don't have preferences, in the rational choice sense, about how to trade off the present for the future. We can't rank different paths in a coherent way, since we always change our plans—unless we somehow shackle our future selves to a path against their wishes, and why would we want to do that? The "choice" of a path that we know we won't stick to isn't really a choice.

Thus we need to think about intertemporal choice in a new way. This type of choice can't be described as purposeful because we lack true preferences. It must not be the case, then, that each moment is tied to an optimal plan that we select and then execute. Neoclassical economic theory cannot account for planning through time; moreover, our sense of choosing in a purposeful way is often illusory. Whether you're a hippie or Zen master professing to live in "the now" or a wealthy miser who takes pride in delaying gratification, each moment necessarily stands for itself.

Choosing across Time Involves a Contradiction

Is planning for the future, deciding when to do what, similar to selecting a consumer good? That is, do we mentally line up all available options and pick the one that's best? In the case of a consumption plan—this much for today, this much for next week, next month, next year—that would mean picking the pattern that provides the best combination of current well-being and anticipated future well-being. Most economists would say, yes, that's what we do, and many non-economists would probably agree.

Time

Let's consider the problem abstractly. To apply rational choice to planning as we did to renting an apartment, we must (1) pick the path that balances our desire to enjoy ourselves now and provide enjoyment for the future, and (2) willingly stay on that path as time passes. The trouble is, (1) and (2) can't coexist because our future selves will care about *their* futures with an intensity comparable to our direct concern about the future from today's point of view. Nearly any way we define the problem, we'll arrive at a contradiction. Assuming people enjoy both consuming and anticipating their future well-being, they will want to change their former plans when the imagined future turns into the present. This is not a statement about "weakness of the will" or human psychology; all conscious beings, even those living on distant planets, are subject to the same mathematics and therefore experience the immediate present in a different way than the imagined future. My aim is not to replace the old calculus with a new one but rather to show that no calculus is going to work.

Although a mathematical proof is necessary to make this argument with precision, it's possible to follow the logic without the math. To see why there can be no stable plan for consuming over time, we will consider two cases. In the first, people look ahead two or more time periods. These periods can be expressed in any units—days, weeks, months, or years. If people are free to change their minds and derive well-being from thinking about how their future selves will obtain pleasure from thinking about *their* futures, they will not stick with any single plan. In the second case, people look ahead only one period. Here, it's possible to arrive at a model that accords with rational choice and leads to a consistent plan over time, but only by performing bizarre and implausible mental feats.

Both cases operate under the most stripped-down set of assumptions—perfect certainty and one type of consumption. If rational choice can't be made to fit in even these simple conditions, think how confused it would become if more realism were introduced to the model with factors like technological progress, social change, or uncertainty about lifespan, health, income, and interest rates.

We conclude from all this that purposeful choice simply does not apply to planning over time if people are able to reevaluate. This doesn't make them irrational, and moreover, it's not even problematic. Some things just can't be crammed into the purposeful choice framework. We can't choose what we prefer among available plans because "prefer" loses its meaning when options refer to different paths in the future.

Looking Ahead More than One Period

According to purposeful choice, everything is commensurable. That is, everything can be translated into a common currency (for instance, money, hours worked), then compared and evaluated. The price of leisure, at this high level of abstraction, is the agent's wage—he "purchases" an hour of leisure by working one hour less. He frames each situation as an optimization problem, then finds the solution that maximizes utility subject to constraints. Since everything has a price, we're justified in aggregating all the inputs into utility and calling that aggregate "consumption," the more the better.

Suppose a person assumes that he will stick to whatever plan he sets, then tries to figure out how to maximize well-being at each point in time, considering the satisfaction he will enjoy from consuming in each period plus satisfaction from anticipating the future. This problem, from today's point of view, should have a solution—some array of consumption should look best. But as long as the person looks more than one period into the future, he will want to deviate from the plan he set out previously.[1] The assumption that he'll stick with the plan cannot hold. Moreover, as a rational actor, he must have known all along that he wouldn't voluntarily stick to the plan, so his assumption was spurious, and it wasn't much of a plan in the first place.

To be a bit more precise, consider someone who derives pleasure on Monday both from consuming and from anticipating his well-being on Tuesday, Wednesday, and beyond. On Monday, he maps out a consumption plan. From the vantage point of Monday, he anticipates his consumption on Tuesday and Wednesday and can also anticipate the pleasure he will feel on Tuesday from anticipating Wednesday. Consumption planned for Wednesday will make him feel more secure on both of the first two days of the week.

Now imagine that a day passes and Tuesday becomes the present. The appeal of Wednesday's consumption must erode relative to Tuesday's. Intuitively, Wednesday's consumption becomes less desirable because the person can only anticipate it once, while Tuesday's consumption becomes more desirable than it appeared on Monday. Why? On Tuesday, even though he loses the benefit of anticipating Tuesday's consumption, he gets to consume it. On the margin, that actual consumption must be at least as satisfying as anticipation was back on Monday. Otherwise there's no hope of a stable solution—he'd perpetually tease himself by anticipating a binge of consumption that he'd flip forward as soon as the time came to partake. As a result of these fluctuating valuations, when Tuesday arrives, the person shifts some of the consumption planned for Wednesday to Tuesday.

As long as today's plan looks more than one period into the future, we find ourselves with a contradiction. No plan that appears optimal in the present will look optimal once the future becomes the present. Simply put, we cannot choose what feels best in each period, including the positive or negative pleasures of anticipating the future, without getting tied up in a knot.[2]

Looking Ahead One Period Only

If people looked ahead only one period, it would be possible to find a solution that is consistent with rational choice, although the underlying assumptions are unappealing. To see why, suppose well-being at any one time depends on the satisfaction a person experiences from consumption in the present plus the well-being she expects in the next period, divided by a factor of $1 + \rho$. In this case, ρ is a psychological constant that represents the trade-off between satisfaction today and satisfaction tomorrow. If we care less about the future than the present, whether the future involves a reward or a punishment, then we underweight the future and ρ is a positive number. By contrast, if we innately cared more about the future, then ρ would be negative but larger than -1.

To achieve a result that is consistent over time, the individual must do three things in the present, which we'll say is Monday. She must hold in her mind the way she expects to feel on Tuesday, Wednesday, and beyond; she must imagine how her consumption flow will appear from the perspective of Tuesday, since her concern for Wednesday operates exclusively through her concern for Tuesday; and she must choose what she prefers after carefully purging from her mind any *direct* concern for Wednesday. That is, Wednesday's consumption enters into her plan only because she cares about Tuesday's iteration of herself and knows that Tuesday's iteration will care about Wednesday's.[3]

If these mental acrobatics seem like a strange account of how we plan for the future, consider further that the three requirements must be applied to one and only one time scale. If a plan holds for units expressed in days, it does not hold for months. That is, Monday's self cares about Tuesday's self, but not directly about Wednesday's self except to the extent that she knows

Wednesday's welfare will be an input into Tuesday's. In this case, however, January, February, and March will obey no such relationship.[4]

One More Way Out . . . Maybe

Let's say you're desperate to find a way to understand time in terms of rational choice. There's one more approach you can take, but you're going to have to make two assumptions and, on close inspection, you're not going to like them.

First, when you think about the future, you must think only about consumption and not how you'll feel about the arrangement that prevails at different points in time. For this model to work, even if the consumption plan you set in April leaves you to starve in June, you must ignore the distress you'll feel about it in May. It's a peculiar assumption, especially since you're already displaying concern about the future by postponing consumption.

Second, you must assume that everyone in the world shares the same innate taste for trading off present satisfaction for future satisfaction, and that this taste happens to be described by one particular mathematical formula. This is another peculiar assumption because there's no reason to think that human nature coincides with the one formula that's compatible with rational choice.[5]

An economist trying to apply rational choice to planning has got a problem. She can go in one of three directions to construct a time-consistent model from first principles: (1) assume individuals have only one shot to plan their lives (the moment the economist is observing them), a perfect ability to bind themselves to that plan, and a desire to compel their future selves to do things those future selves might not wish to do; (2) assume individuals can look only one period ahead and that there is a single natural time scale for planning; or (3) assume individuals care about only present and future consumption and not how they will feel in the future, and that they coincidentally discount satisfaction from future consumption according to the one formula that works mathematically.

When their models fail to describe actual behavior, economists resort to blaming the cognitive bias known as "hyperbolic discounting."[6] This so-called bias leads to preferences that are "time-inconsistent," meaning we can't set a plan and then stick to it. But are "time-inconsistent" preferences really preferences at all? Preferences hinge on the ability to rank options, but we can't rank options here. In fact, we can't even choose, in any meaningful sense, a path, since we can't commit our future selves to staying on it. Rather than a consequence of cognitive bias, "time-inconsistent preferences" is an oxymoron.

The realization that people cannot exhibit true preferences over the timing of their consumption is no cause for a crisis in our understanding of the human condition. A lack of such preferences won't get me into trouble. The analog to time-inconsistent preferences in more static choices would be "intransitive preferences." These are genuinely bad. Suppose I prefer strawberry ice

cream to chocolate, given a choice between the two, and simultaneously prefer chocolate to vanilla and vanilla to strawberry. I
could then fall victim to the famous "money pump": a wise guy
could give me chocolate for free, charge me to switch to strawberry (which I prefer), charge me again to switch to vanilla
(which I prefer to strawberry), then charge me to switch to
chocolate. If those were truly my preferences, he'd continue
like that until he'd pumped out all my money. Yet holding "time-
inconsistent preferences," that is, wanting out of the plan the enforcement demon and I agreed to, causes no corresponding bad
thing to happen. That's because enforcement demons don't exist.

Is the entire argument that there can be no time-consistent
plan really just a fancy way of saying that life is a journey—a
sentiment so tired it appears on greeting cards? Perhaps, but no
greeting card explains why life should be conceived of as a journey rather than a sequence of destinations over which we have
well-defined preferences.

Fooling Ourselves

As we've just discussed, intertemporal planning cannot be made
to fit into rational choice. The fact that we change our minds
may seem natural and self-evident to those who take life as it
comes, as if playing a game. Others (like me) may find this more
difficult to see. It can be especially difficult since rational choice
gives us license to wait until *after* we act to ferret out our motives. If my wife asks why I failed to stop at the store on my way

home, I can list reasons why it made sense to shop later. She might then ask, "Did you actually think through those reasons at the time?" But that's not a serious challenge to my belief that I paid attention to her request. For my story to hold water and for me to feel truthful in the telling, I don't need to claim or believe that the explanation came up to my consciousness.

Lately, I've been studying Japanese a little bit each day, a project that makes no sense. I was never that good at it when I heard it all day working at a Japanese bank and have little talent for foreign languages in general. I have no need for it in my life—if I'm lucky, I'll get to go to Japan on business once a year, and everyone I meet there speaks English. Plenty of interesting subjects would be easier to learn and more relevant to my life.

Yet, if probed, I could rattle off reasons why this is a sound idea. For instance, it's efficient to spend a relatively small amount of time to preserve what little Japanese I still know before it all slips away, it's good for mental agility, and so on. (I wouldn't say I find the studying pleasant because I experience it as a chore.) Rational choice theory doesn't require that actors be aware of *how* their behavior optimizes, so long as it does. Perhaps my slow, casual study of Japanese really is rational, but I suspect it's not. It feels more like a small challenge I've undertaken for its own sake.

Attributing motives to our own actions comes naturally. Psychological studies have demonstrated that people cook up explanations when none are readily available. One well-known

experiment was conducted on a "split-brain" patient whose cor-
pus callosum, the bundle of fibers connecting the right cerebral
hemisphere to the left, had been severed to control epilepsy. A
card with "Walk" written on it was shown to the patient in such
a way that only the right cerebral hemisphere received the instruction. He began walking. When the researcher asked the
subject why he was walking, the answer could only come from
the left side of his brain, the seat of language. Since the left hemisphere was unable to communicate with the right, the left did
not know that he was following a written instruction. The subject replied: "I wanted to get a Coke." The researcher was convinced that the subject genuinely believed his explanation.[7]

This process may be observable even at the neurochemical
level. Neuroscientist Benjamin Libet detected a specific electri-
cal stimulus he called "readiness potential" that fires in the human
brain as much as 350 to 400 milliseconds before subjects become
conscious of their intent to act.[8] While the interpretation of this
study is controversial, it suggests that decisions may be initiated
unconsciously from what Thomas Nagel calls the "blind spot . . .
that hides something we cannot take into account in acting, because it is what acts."[9]

This finding wouldn't have surprised Schopenhauer, who
wrote that "men are only apparently drawn from in front; really they are pushed from behind."[10] I wouldn't go so far as to
argue that this is always the case or to stake out the extreme
position that reason is strictly a slave to passion and that we're

forever deluding ourselves about our motives. Often, reason and passion work together, just as rational choice assumes. But at other times, it only feels that way.

Discounting and Double Counting

Before moving on to an alternative, for-itself account of action over time, let's look at a quick example that illustrates how reflexively treating choice over time like any other choice can lead to confusion.

Eating gave pleasure to humans before they understood anything about nutrition. Now we value both the pleasure of eating and nutrition. These benefits can be added together. When deciding what to eat, we weigh the combined benefits against the expense and various health concerns. Let's say I'm serving myself chili from a large kettle and can take as much as I want for free. If I don't like chili but I'm hungry, I'll eat a little. If I'm not hungry but like the taste, I'll again eat a little. If I'm hungry and love chili, I'll eat more than in either of the previous cases. It's straightforward—we live to eat and eat to live.

But it's not so straightforward with a similar choice involving time in a puzzle posed by the philosopher Robert Nozick, who posits an evolutionary basis for discounting the future. In his analysis, if primitive humans had a 2 percent chance of dying each year, those who unconsciously discounted by about 2 percent per year when saving for the future (in their way) could have enjoyed a survival advantage. They would then have passed this present-mindedness on to their descendants, endowing modern humans with the same tendency to discount the future.[11] (Never mind whether any of this sociobiology is true. We're interested in the theoretical problem that arises from misclassifying the present-versus-future trade-off as purposeful choice.) Since we pick present-oriented paths, such as 101 units today and 99 tomorrow rather than 100 units each day, it may appear that we *desire* to discount the future.

Thanks to language and actuarial tables, we can now consciously reflect on the future in ways our ancestors could not. If there's a 98 percent chance we'll be around next year, we should discount expected consumption by 2 percent, holding everything else equal. (Assume for the sake of this puzzle that modern humans care only about consumption that occurs in their own lifetime and do not save money to bequeath to descendants or charity.) Yet we were already discounting by 2 percent because of our inherited cognitive apparatus. It feels wrong to combine the innate "desire" to discount (analogous to the pleasure of eating) with survival calculations (analogous to the nutritional value of food) and discount the future by 4 percent. One could argue that going with 2 percent instead maximizes expected consumption given survival probabilities and simultaneously satisfies our desire to discount. But is it right to double count 2 percent discounting, allowing it to satisfy two different "motives" at once?

Nozick concedes that "the situation is . . . complicated."[12] Yet no one would suggest that a person who is hungry has to solve a brainteaser to know what to do. This puzzle arises from mistaking intertemporal choice for a preference that can be added together with other preferences. Satisfying hunger and obtaining nourishment are inputs into our utility function; discounting the future is not. Nor is it a desire that can be traded off for, or combined with, other desires.

The answer to the puzzle, then, is: no, don't add the two factors together. A person who expects to live a long time might be frugal and discount by 2 percent, but if he learns he's about to die, he might logically wish to abandon his previous plan and live it up.

9

Homo Economicus *and* Homo Ludens

A few years ago, I joined a game of football in Central Park with strangers. The teams were evenly matched. While the game was under way, both sides wanted to win. But why did they care? Why did I? I had never seen my teammates or opponents before and would never see them again. There was no prize for winning, no lasting increase in status. During that hour, my experience was essentially dynamic. I was caught in the flow, seeking victory. Shortly after the game was over, I forgot the final score.

According to rational choice, I should have been willing to trade victory at some rate of exchange. So how much would I have paid for a touchdown? The truth is that even if I could have paid a sum of money to guarantee victory without anyone knowing, I wouldn't have considered it. Victory in that game couldn't have been meaningfully traded off for other things. But although

I couldn't have put a price on winning, it wasn't some priceless treasure that transcends money, like the lives of my children. It was an essentially arbitrary aim that only mattered while the process was taking place. The point was not to win, but to struggle to win and meet each new challenge as it arose. For a professional football player, winning may be purposeful because it maximizes his earning prospects. But if he also loves to play and forgets about the money in the middle of a game, then he is not merely optimizing.

I am aware that there is a price for nearly everything, including the outcome of a low-stakes football game. If a top-hatted man had interrupted the game to offer me $1 million to lose intentionally and I trusted that he was not playing a trick, I would have taken the money. (I would also have thrown the game for considerably less than that, of course.) Apart from the $1 million, engaging with this odd benefactor would be a kind of adventure, a game of its own. I'd want to take the money to see what it was all about. But this sort of offer doesn't usually arise, and since I am interested in explaining everyday activity, this thought experiment doesn't tell us much.

While the Central Park football game unfolded, my interest in winning couldn't be shoehorned into purposeful choice. As we saw in Chapter 8, no sensible model leads to "preferences" for different paths through time, even given perfect information about the future. A come-from-behind victory in my football game might have been in some sense better than winning easily, and winning easily would be better than losing, but "better" doesn't really apply here because the different paths can't be ranked.

Before the mathematization of economics in the mid-twentieth century, it was not radical for economists to recognize that people care about the process as well as results.[1] By this, the economists didn't mean some version of what we now call cognitive bias—the manufacturer whom Alfred Marshall described in Chapter 2 as motivated more by the pursuit of victory than increasing his wealth is not making a mistake.[2]

Thorstein Veblen pointed out that rational choice (or "marginal utility theory," as he called it) "offers no theory of a movement of any kind, being occupied with the adjustment of values to a given situation . . . For all their use of the term 'dynamic,' neither Mr. [John Bates] Clark nor any of his associates in this line of research have yet contributed anything at all appreciable to a theory of genesis, growth, sequence, change, process, or the like, in economic life."[3] "Genesis, growth, sequence, change, [and] process" are not minor matters; they are fundamental to our experience. An additional theory is needed to stand alongside purposeful choice and address those facets of life that it ignores.

Johan Huizinga's *Homo ludens*, the playing/sporting human, in contrast to *Homo economicus*, embodies Keynes's view of time as "organic rather than atomistic."[4] Huizinga defined play as "a free activity . . . connected with no material interest . . . It proceeds within its own proper boundaries of time and space according to fixed rules and in an orderly manner."[5] Dancing would be an equally good metaphor. Huizinga frames action as a continuous flow rather than a sequence of discrete moments. Instead of adhering to plans that are dictated by preferences, the *Homo ludens* chooses how to respond to new scenarios as they arise and which challenges to tackle. These choices and the ensuing struggle are for-itself.

This depiction of choice through time shares elements with prospect theory, an influential thrust of behavioral economics. In 1979, Daniel Kahneman and Amos Tversky proposed this psychological account of various anomalies such as the tendency to become more risk averse when confronting small losses rather than small gains or to take inordinate risks to earn back previous losses. According to prospect theory, a person facing choice under uncertainty begins by computing a base-case outcome or reference point, then characterizes each outcome as a gain or loss relative to that reference point. As in for-itself choosing, in prospect theory the status quo anchors decisions no matter the circumstances or probabilities, and the decision-maker pushes ahead from there.

Because prospect theory assumes that choices are fully determined by preferences, however, it cannot provide a dynamic account of how individuals navigate through time. Nor does it allow for unpredictable behavior. In the for-itself framework, choosing involves will, so observers cannot predict precisely which challenges people will embrace.

For-Itself Action Involves Free Choice

At some point, we must stop calculating and act. Keynes attributed this "spontaneous urge to action" to "animal spirits."[6] By this he meant much more than "irrational exuberance." He meant instead the exercise of will that lies at the heart of all action.[7] Rational choice economics allows for no such spirits: choice happens automatically within a world the individual did not create. The individual encounters only the outcome. But these spirits are at home within for-itself theory, in which the act of choosing, of overcoming the state of indeterminacy that prevails before the choice is made, is crucial and the outcome often less important than we might imagine.

This is not to say that the way a choice is made can never matter in the purposeful realm. It can, in the service of self-interest. In the Western movie *Shane*, Joe Starrett tries to drive Shane off his land. Shane says he'll leave after Starrett puts down his gun. Starrett asks what difference it makes when Shane is leaving anyway. Shane answers, "I'd like it to be my idea." Shane, a tough guy, cares about how he leaves. He's better off proving that he can't be pushed around. Meek, polite people, too, can care about how choices are made. In an example from Amartya Sen, you want to sit in the most comfortable chair at a garden party but don't want to be a "chair grabber."[8] You'll sit there only if the host insists. You'd like it *not* to be your idea.

These calculated choices contrast with true acts of will, which are experienced as free. They are not dictated by preexisting preferences or an authority who oppresses us. Of course, this freedom isn't absolute, since we always face rules and constraints to varying degrees. Chess is no fun unless you play strictly by the book, but in a friendly baseball game, there's a lot of leeway for adapting rules to the conditions and number of players.[9]

Consumers, too, operate within constraints but still want to feel that their decisions arise without coercion. A good salesperson does not push too hard or seek to rob the consumer of the experience of choice. Perhaps this is why ads don't generally focus on conveying information that makes an airtight case for the product. Singers on a hilltop belting out "I'd like to buy the world a Coke" sell more soda than a clear presentation of product information, for example, that consumers prefer Coke in taste tests, that you can pour it in a glass with a scoop of ice cream, and so on. No one wants an open-and-shut case: that would leave no room for the exercise of will. So sellers remind consumers that the product exists, then let their reason be a slave to their passions. The "soft sell" allows prospective buyers to connect the dots. This applies in other arenas as well—in movies, and perhaps in real life, people rebel against the romantic interest who seems too perfect. (The extreme case of the soft sell is the anti-sell, in which customers are actively discouraged. Bernie Madoff was famously a master of this dark art.)

Parents try to stake out the middle ground that allows children to choose freely which challenges to pursue, while steering them clear of mistakes. After graduating from college with a degree in archaeology and anthropology, my daughter, Alice, asked me which career was best. Did she need to work at a not-for-profit to be a good person? The second question was relatively easy. I told her about the butcher, the brewer, and the baker. As Adam Smith said in the most famous passage in all of economics, it's not by their benevolence "that we expect our dinner, but from their regard to their own interest."[10] If she's drawn to work in the private sector, that's what she should do.

But I recognized the dangers of going beyond that to address which career would be best. If Alice chose out of a desire to please me and it turned out badly, she might resent my interference. Plus, she was more likely to excel if she followed an independent desire. Both of these reasons can be understood as purposeful—by staying out of it, I avoid the risk of harming our relationship and actually help Alice achieve a better career outcome. But there's more. It would be a mistake to subordinate the act of choosing to the outcome. The choice is personal, and she must make it on her own if the challenges she faces are to feel authentic.

For-itself choice must be free, but this is not to say that we pick challenges at random or that for-itself choice operates completely outside of rationality. While I was playing the football game described earlier, I chose continuously, trying to overcome obstacles by running the most effective plays. The game was for-itself, but my tactics in pursuit of victory were rational.

Whether the challenges we face are important or trivial, the experience of freely and actively choosing is fundamental to for-itself action over time. This contrasts with the purposeful realm where choice is like digestion—reflexive and only noticed when it appears to be malfunctioning. This limited view of choice has unfairly loaded it with negative baggage, creating a false impression of paradox and cognitive bias, as the following puzzles demonstrate.

Two Puzzles

Consider, first, the view that too much choice is unsettling to consumers, as Barry Schwartz argues in *The Paradox of Choice*.

Eating out can be a minefield of choice. A survey of 830 American menus posted online found an average of 114 items offered at each restaurant. Although voluminous menus aren't new (an 1899 Delmonico's menu listed thirty-five dishes in the vegetable category alone), it is sometimes criticized as a curse of modern life, a pathology of free markets.[11]

But if the average consumer dislikes excessive variety, why does it exist? The profit motive should drive it out, since the market has every incentive to meet our needs subject to cost. Consumers who find lengthy menus overwhelming should be willing to pay for a simpler experience, allowing restaurateurs to earn an above-market profit by limiting options. A half-dozen items on a menu should satisfy customers' appetites and food tolerances, and shrinking the menu would allow a restaurant to increase turnover and hence freshness while holding down costs.

But this must not be what the average consumer demands. Perhaps customers are happy to sacrifice price and quality and engage with a confusing menu in order to exercise their ability to choose. Rather than a nuisance, choice is crucial to enjoying the meal.

At large drugstores, consumers encounter an even greater abundance of options, and some complain about having to contend with a hundred brands of toothpaste. But perhaps some consumers actually enjoy engaging with dizzying choice and complain mostly to preserve their self-image as rational. It would be a big deal to many people if a store offered only one brand of toothpaste, even if in a blind taste test no one could tell the difference. If a store failed to provide sufficient options, they would shop elsewhere.

But what, then, of all the research "proving" that people dislike too much choice? In one well-known study, disguised research assistants set up two types of tasting stands in grocery stores. At one stand, shoppers were invited to sample six kinds of jam, while at the second, they were invited to sample twenty-four. Shoppers who were exposed to fewer choices were more likely to purchase a jar of jam.[12] But an aversion to excessive jam options doesn't necessarily mean that people dislike choice. They just don't want to engage with too many options or waste too much time relative to the matter at hand—after all, it's only jam. In any case, this experiment tells us little about the real world where merchants learn to offer only as many options as consumers want to analyze.

I trust my belief that profit-maximizing merchants know what they are doing over an intuition that consumers truly prefer less variety. While anxiety may accompany choice, consumers evidently want to experience this anxiety and its subsequent release once the choice is made. Are we drawn to movies in which only good fortune befalls the protagonist? Of course not. Enjoying a dramatic plot with a buildup of tension is no more paradoxical than the paradox of choice.

The second puzzle is called the "disjunction effect." It occurs when someone can't act until he determines his motive, even if all possible motives justify the same action. It is supposed to represent a deviation from rationality.

Amos Tversky and Eldar Shafir coined "disjunction effect" after conducting the following experiment: undergraduates are told to imagine that they have just taken a grueling qualifying exam. They will learn the next day, before the winter holiday, whether they passed or failed. They can buy a five-day vacation to Hawaii at an exceptionally low price today, pay a small nonrefundable fee for the option of buying the trip in two days when they know the exam results, or pass up the opportunity altogether.

A student could decide to buy the vacation out of two very different motives. If she passes the exam, she might want to go to Hawaii to celebrate. If she fails, she might want to go to console herself.

Out of sixty-six students, 32 percent said they would buy the vacation, 7 percent would not, and 61 percent would pay the fee to wait. In a second version of the experiment, students were asked whether they would buy the trip if they passed the exam and whether they would buy the trip if they failed. Two-thirds of the students made the same decision regardless of the exam outcome.[13]

Under rational choice, in which students care about only the costs and benefits of the vacation, too many in the first version of the experiment paid to wait to discover their motives. They paid for information they did not need, since passing and failing both lead to the same choice. Were they behaving irrationally? If we accept that the choice for-itself matters, then the answer is no. The students wanted to be able to make their own choice of whether to celebrate or console themselves.

While paying to wait is, in a sense, a waste of money, students suffering the disjunction effect have my sympathy. I'd probably behave the same way. The choice to celebrate feels substantively different than the choice to restore my spirits. I'd like to leave the version of myself who passes the exam free to celebrate and the version who fails free to go to Hawaii to plot his comeback. The act of choosing could be as important as the outcome.

It would be interesting to conduct a less emotionally charged version of this experiment, subjecting students to uncertainty of a more mundane sort. For example, they could be presented with the same options and learn tomorrow whether or not a family reunion is taking place in Hawaii. They are waiting not for exam results but for relatives to sort out their schedules. I would bet that fewer students who are going to Hawaii one way or another— whether to join a family reunion or on their own—would pay to postpone that decision.

The Art of Crafting Meaningful Challenges

There is an art to seizing a goal and giving it meaning, suppressing any recognition that overcoming today's seemingly critical challenge won't matter in the long run. We let alternative challenges percolate in the background, ready when needed. If none are pressing (or tempting), the current task expands to the time allotted. When we start to reach our goal, well that's fine, but we quickly discover that what we really want is whatever comes next. Ideally, we transition to the next pursuit without feeling like a horse chasing a carrot suspended in front of its nose. So long as the challenges meet certain standards, we can remain engaged in the chase.

Challenges Must Be (or Feel) Authentic

In the for-itself framework, people navigate through time by choosing challenges consciously or unconsciously and struggling to overcome them. Obstacles may be physical or mental, daunting or relatively easy. Regardless of its specific characteristics, the challenge must arise authentically for people to willingly engage. To feel authentic, hurdles must have a natural meaning in our lives. They cannot feel entirely concocted or externally imposed.

Sometimes, when genuine obstacles are scarce, we gamify our lives to allow for a struggle that feels meaningful—100 percent authenticity is not the standard. At these times, we make things harder for ourselves to combat potential tedium.

Procrastination is a handy technique for upping the stakes. To those who don't engage in it, procrastination looks like a character flaw. From a rational choice perspective, it should not exist. If people continuously reevaluated their activities to maximize gratification from consumption, there could be no procrastination. We would lay out all our tasks and perform each at the optimal time. We wouldn't postpone health care until the symptoms of disease flared up, since no rational calculation could justify skipping routine checkups. My students wouldn't be up late cramming the night before the exam, and I wouldn't be up late writing the questions.

Yet almost all of us at least occasionally wait until the last minute, when the penalty for failing to act becomes more severe. Postponing a task right up to the deadline is exciting: we need to feel the bite before it rises to the level of a game worth playing.

I don't want to suggest that procrastination is a strategy for harnessing occult powers of "good stress" that appear to the procrastinator if he waits long enough. Dull tasks are simply more attractive under time pressure, whether or not that pressure generates better results. If our true motives for postponing strike us as contrived, we tell ourselves a story. We either invent a reason that the activity had to be postponed until the last minute or shrug and diagnose ourselves with an unfortunate character trait that results in chronic delay.

One might also rationalize procrastination by saying, "Oh well, I'm just very present oriented; I heavily discount the future." That, too, is a delusion. A student might delay writing a paper for a week, raising the cost in some sense by 20 percent, but refuse to borrow money at an interest rate of 20 percent per week. That student is "present oriented" only with respect to a specific task—which is another way of saying that she procrastinates.

Challenges that result from procrastination aren't perfectly authentic. We *choose* to let time pressure build, but because it happens naturally, it may not strike us as entirely bogus. In the absence of true obstacles, we construct makeshift challenges and strain to give them a veneer of authenticity.

In some cases, groups act together to reinforce a contrived sense of authenticity. In recent years, long walks for charity have become popular. Why don't the walkers spend that time working or engaged in some more pleasant pastime? They could donate half their earnings or half the value of the extra leisure and everyone would gain. But clearly, participants enjoy linking the walk-a-thon to the cause they support. While walk-a-thons may seem artificial and useless to some, for others they instill physical struggle with meaning. This craving for authentic physical challenges that for many are absent from modern life can also explain extremes in exercise, sports, all-nighters at the office, political campaigns, military training, and prodigious work travel.

Businesses may deliberately make experiences harder than necessary for consumers. "Why don't they just raise the price?" the economist asks in response to long lines at popular restaurants and sporting events. The restaurant owner who could reduce lines by raising prices might instead reinforce the authenticity of the waiting line by citing a motive other than profit maximization, such as fair pricing. Whatever the owner's motive, for the consumer, the fight is part of the product and part of its appeal.

Players Must Stay in the Game

Suppose you suddenly and unexpectedly receive a significant amount of money. Would you act with caution and set the whole amount aside? Or would you throw caution to the wind and splurge? Rational choice predicts that people would save most of a financial windfall and spread the benefits over their lifetime. They would raise their standard of living permanently, hence the "permanent income hypothesis." Yet few who obtain a one-off payment spend it on an annuity that provides a constant income stream. This suggests that few people truly want to feather their nests enough to settle into steady gratification through consumption and leisure for the rest of their lives—that would deprive future years of challenge. Better to save some, spend some, and leave room to grow in the future. Spending now may look like impatience but is in a sense the opposite: excessive caution today would spoil tomorrow's fun.[14]

Similarly, many who become rich continue taking financial

and business risks even when there is a chance those risks will make them poor again. If a risk pans out, they have overcome a challenge. If it doesn't, they have created a fresh opportunity to rebuild.

To avoid reaching the endpoint too soon, we might prolong a challenge at the expense of the formal objective. Boxers dominating a fight may fail to finish off their opponents in order to savor the win. An experiment reported in the journal *Econometrica* documented a more mundane example of players who sacrifice winnings to stay in the game. Experimental subjects playing computer games in a lab chose a strategy and watched their winnings increase or decrease over time. If their winnings dropped below a threshold, they became bankrupt, and their payoff would be zero. The subjects ended up selecting strategies that kept them alive in the game but lowered their expected payout. The author interprets this as evidence that a "deeply ingrained (and usually reliable) heuristic towards survival leads subjects to associate survival with optimality." On this basis, he speculates that real-world managers conduct business too conservatively if they suffer from "survival bias."[15] Maybe. But I can imagine myself behaving like the experimental subjects, particularly since they couldn't leave the lab early and the amount of money at stake was only a few dollars. Watching after I'd been eliminated would be boring, so I'd forgo a payout to stay in the game.

In *Life of Alexander*, Plutarch describes Alexander the Great grappling with this conundrum:

Whenever he heard Philip [II of Macedon] had taken any town of importance, or won any signal victory, instead of rejoicing at it altogether, he would tell his companions that his father would anticipate everything, and leave him and them no opportunities of performing great and illustrious actions. For being more bent upon action and glory than either upon pleasure or riches, he esteemed all that he should receive from his father as a diminution and prevention of his own future achievements; and would have chosen rather to succeed to a kingdom involved in troubles and wars, which would have afforded him frequent exercise of his courage, and a large field of honour, than to one already flourishing and settled, where his inheritance would be an inactive life, and the mere enjoyment of wealth and luxury.[16]

Alexander was happy to inherit the throne—he didn't object to unearned privilege as a matter of principle—but he was loath to inherit a kingdom so secure that it would deprive him of challenges.

Outcomes Must Be Uncertain

A challenge can't be genuine if success is guaranteed—you've got to wrestle with elements that can't be foreseen or controlled. The successes we remember are close calls that work out in the end. (I hesitate to call these the "best," since that implies comparison and ranking, which are not part of the for-itself realm.) I grappled with just such a challenge when the United Kingdom voted to drop out of the European Union in June 2016.

I had an ominous feeling in the lead-up to the Brexit referendum, although I can't say I expected the Leave camp to win.

Anyone who claims to have seen it coming is kidding themselves. The vote in favor of withdrawing from the European Union was, objectively, shocking. Our hedge fund had a lot riding on the vote, more than we would have liked. A Brexit shock could plunge markets into chaos, right when we were counting on investors to follow through on commitments to supply capital. If investors responded by freezing up, we would be unable to pay for the deals to which the funds had committed.

Three transactions were scheduled to settle between June 30 and July 5—an unusual concentration. We had agreed with two banks in Italy and one in Germany to invest a total of €550 million in structured deals that would transfer risk to our funds and boost the banks' capital ratios. The settlements centered around June 30 because the banks needed to reflect these investments on their quarterly financial statements.

The money in our funds doesn't slosh around waiting for us to put it to work. Rather, we call the capital from investors bit by bit when we're ready. Even if they've made a legally binding commitment, we won't force them to do something they don't want to do. We bite our tongues and say: "Okay, we want you to be comfortable." We do not push too hard, nor do we argue: "We are counting on this money. The banks are counting on it. If you back out, you're jeopardizing our business and our future." That kind of pressure isn't what our investors signed on for.

On the evening of the vote, June 23, I tried to reassure myself that the capital calls wouldn't present a problem, since all signs pointed toward victory for Remain. Exit polls were favorable and the British pound had rallied sharply. Nigel Farage, a leader of the Leave campaign, even conceded defeat. Still, I couldn't sleep. And around 1:00 a.m. in London, the results started to point to a win for Leave.

The morning after the vote, I jogged around Hyde Park and Kensington Gardens. Normally, I find jogging excruciating and count down the minutes until the torture will end. That day, I didn't even notice. My pain was crowded out by the looming horror.

In finance, as in many other fields, you sometimes make promises you might not be able to keep. If you rely on others, they might let you down, forcing you to relay your disappointment down the line. You can apply pressure. You can take evasive action. But eventually, if you run out of tricks, there's nothing left to do but apologize to those who were depending on you.

Apologies won't prevent a blow to your reputation, however. If we failed to settle one trade with a bank, that bank's board of directors would never commit to us again. Word would spread to other banks. In this case, we could try to blame the shock of Brexit, but the stain on our reputation would still be long-lasting.

Later, but still quite early that Friday morning, my business partners and I met in a semi-secret interior room in our London office for a grown-up conversation. If investors backed out, where could we find more money on such short notice? If we couldn't find it, which bank should we stiff? Of the three banks that were counting on us, which would be hurt the most? Could we scale down any of the transactions without obtaining new regulatory approvals? Which banks could have picked another investor and thus would feel especially wronged if we couldn't fulfill our commitment? Where did we have personal relationships strong enough to sustain a failure of this magnitude? If we delayed settlement, would it be better to notify the bank in advance, or to fail and ask for forgiveness after? If we delayed for a few days, would the bank still be able to account for the deal as if it had settled by the end of the quarter?

Together, my partners and I had been through the 1997–1998 Asian crisis, the Lehman crisis, and plenty of idiosyncratic crises in between. We knew ourselves and we knew each other. We were able to settle on a plan that juggled all the variables, then got to work. After confirming that a few investors wanted to drop out, we decided whom to ask for more money and just what to say to them. At the same time, we explored the consequences of asking for an extension on one of the three transactions.

Our plan worked. We persuaded one defecting investor to reverse course and another large investor to make up the remaining shortfall. (Some investors will help out in a pinch—but better not have too many pinches.) All three bank trades settled on time without a euro to spare. We'd had a little bad luck, then enough good luck to squeak by. We knew that obstacles are not always overcome and crises don't always end happily. We felt gratitude for the investors who came through, relief that disaster had been averted, and satisfaction with the camaraderie of working together and with the investors and banks that relied on us.

I cannot understand these feelings or our Brexit adventure more generally in terms of purposeful choice. Even though I accept that anxiety and that familiar cold sweat are unavoidable when working at a hedge fund, as at many other businesses, I would never have chosen this trial if it were presented to me on a menu of options. Yet now that it's all over, I recognize that I was fully immersed in the action, and that it was more satisfying than anything else I might have been doing at that time.

The seriousness of our Brexit predicament was intrinsic to the excitement of overcoming it. But while facing high-stakes scenarios can make work feel meaningful, it can't be the only way to create that feeling—if it were, we'd all be emergency room doctors or firefighters. Work, then, must provide a sense of meaning in other ways.

Why Do We Work?

Is work really a burden and retirement the reward at the end, the sooner the better? Plenty of evidence suggests that we're not as eager to give up work as we might imagine or pretend. Consider the current global bull market in protectionism. Could this be a widespread failure to grasp David Ricardo's two-hundred-year-old story of the wine maker from Portugal and the cloth maker from England, in which both countries benefit from trading? Of course, English vintners and Portuguese weavers may not benefit, but the gains from trade should be large enough to compensate the losers so that everyone ends up better off.[17]

The Ricardo solution would not satisfy U.S. workers left behind by the loss of manufacturing jobs. These workers are clamoring not for redistribution, but for the return of their jobs.

Worker dissatisfaction with new service jobs or no jobs at all doesn't fit entirely within a rational choice explanation, even if workers are assumed to value pride and challenges alongside material satisfaction. To see why, suppose unemployed factory workers receive a government subsidy equal to their former pay. If the workers are rational and still unhappy with this state of affairs, they should volunteer to work at another job for no pay— that would get them back to their previous hours and wages, which they presumably prefer. But it's unlikely that they'd choose to volunteer at factories.

For-itself theory suggests a simple explanation for unemployed workers who persist in wanting their jobs back despite government retraining programs in the service industry or subsidies to compensate for lost wages. They want to work as they did in the past, overcoming challenges on the factory floor and providing for their families. They want to take pride in making things that society deems important. The jobs were more than means to an end—they constituted part of the workers' identities.

Under this interpretation, arguments against free trade are rationalizations. Accusations like "job stealing" help the fiction stick. Workers happily justify trade barriers, and one more lecture on comparative advantage is unlikely to succeed when all the previous ones have failed. As Frank Knight asked, "Why do economists make themselves absurd or pathetic by 'teaching' the public things they would see without teaching if they were willing, and being unwilling, certainly will not be taught?"[18]

The for-itself idea of action over time as a dynamic, uneven process can also help us understand labor supply in ways that the purposeful model alone cannot. For example, according to purposeful choice, a temporary wage increase induces people to substitute work for time off: leisure becomes more expensive, so people consume less of it. But a permanent wage hike leads to a "wealth effect" that partly crowds out the "substitution effect." Workers are drawn to supply more labor because the wage is higher, but less labor because the high wage makes them richer. In this view, at a sufficiently high wage, workers respond to further raises by supplying less labor. When this happens, economists say that the labor supply is "bending backward." Yet while the U.S. factory workweek has shortened by one-third since 1900, as the purposeful model predicts, long hours are still typical in certain fields with high permanent wages like investment banking and medicine. Why? According to for-itself theory, the number of hours worked by the highest earners in these fields has remained relatively unchanged over time because a higher wage generally corresponds to more engaging work.

What about when wages go down? During recessions, more workers in the United States and other OECD countries withdraw from the labor force than rational choice predicts. This holds true even after taking into account the effect of unemployment benefits.[19] But if the jobs available at lower wages are less engaging, it's not surprising that some workers on the margin retreat from the labor force while looking for jobs that appeal to them.

Redefining the Good Economy

Putting aside how the economy does work, how *should* it work? Recognizing the spiritual importance of work can help us rethink what a good economy is, how it should serve its citizens, and what policies might foster its realization. In purposeful choice, which dominates policy decisions relating to economic matters, an economy is judged to be satisfactory if it produces abundant goods, provides ample leisure, and distributes those goods and leisure without too much inequality.

This model for the good economy sounds about right until taken to its logical conclusion. If the point of work is to afford consumption and leisure, then the very best economy would be one in which no one had to work at all, where computers and robots provided everything anyone could want. In 1930, Keynes famously forecasted that by 2030 advances in technology would mostly take over the work necessary to satisfy absolute needs such as food and shelter; consequently the workday would be cut to three hours. Keynes did acknowledge that work served a second function, allowing high achievers to feel superior to others, but figured that within a hundred years people would find less grubby ways to establish status.[20]

Although Keynes's prediction is unlikely to come true by 2030 (eighty-five years in, one of his grandnephews admitted to working fifteen hours per *day*, "from breakfast till [he] went to bed at night"), his estimate that real incomes would rise by a factor of eight over a hundred years appears to be on track for the most developed countries.[21] But not everyone's absolute needs have been satiated, and new needs, like mobile phones and organic food, have emerged. Additionally, people still crave the forms of competition particular to work.

From the for-itself perspective, a world in which technology provided all our material needs would be not a paradise but a dystopia. A good economy delivers jobs that involve challenges as well as opportunities for self-discovery and problem-solving. My objective is not a brainwashing campaign. I neither expect nor desire my employees to announce on Monday mornings: "TGIM! Now I can return to my job and struggle with challenges alongside my colleagues." Rather, I'm arguing that every job has qualities that we can measure—the wage, benefits, hours, workplace safety, and so on—as well as a non-quantifiable quality. That quality is for-itself.

After a distinguished career of fifty years, Edmund Phelps sat down with a blank piece of paper to work out how an economy might best engage workers. The answer, according to Phelps, lies in a particular type of modern capitalism that he identifies in his book *Mass Flourishing.* That economy is "dynamic." Entrepreneurs and workers test out new ideas, and innovation takes hold at the grassroots. People flourish not only in terms of consumption, but also because "a good economy promotes lives of vitality."[22]

Phelps shows that this dynamism comes not from breakthroughs in basic science, the accumulation of physical capital, human capital (education and training), or the emergence of business geniuses like Bill Gates. If science were enough, dynamic economies would have sprung up at various points in the ancient world. The Greeks, for instance, achieved little by way of business or commercial innovation in spite of their astonishing scientific achievements. Not only did they know that the earth is round, around 240 BCE Eratosthenes calculated its circumference within a few thousand miles. They understood the causes of lunar and solar eclipses and accurately predicted when they would occur. Anaximander, born two hundred years before Aristotle, speculated that life first formed in water. Ancient Romans surmised that disease is caused by invisible little animals—an idea that could have made the Middle Ages considerably more pleasant, if only they had run with it.[23] But unfortunately, most of this science never made it to the shop room floor.[24]

Having examined when commercial activity thrives and when it does not, Phelps concludes in *Mass Flourishing*, daringly for an economist, that values play a central role. Values determine the extent to which people, whether swashbuckling entrepreneurs or staffers in established firms, pour their energies into business. Certain values give rise to an entrepreneurial spirit that seizes particular ages, including Britain starting in 1815; the United States, Belgium, and France starting in the 1830s; and Germany and Prussia in the second half of the nineteenth century. This spirit is necessary for mass flourishing.

While mass flourishing is a social phenomenon fostered by common values, each person's engagement within a dynamic economy is necessarily for-itself. The values that prompt people to take up challenges are more elusive than traditional inputs into society's production function, yet as Phelps argues, they can still be studied and gradually understood. Employees and entrepreneurs caught up in the "sport" of economic life supply agile thinking and take risks, feeding into the innovation crucial to the good economy. That economy in turn makes rewarding jobs broadly accessible—not only to those with the skill set to become robotics engineers in Silicon Valley, but also to those whose work depends on muscle, sociability, organizational skills, and practical cleverness.

Not long ago, the line between sports and work could become quite blurred. In *American Work-Sports*, Frank Zarnowski documents the number-one team sport in America in the 1850s, after cricket faded and before baseball took hold: the firemen's muster. Firemen would compete in tournaments with standardized rules, mostly as to how far and how high they could pump water. Firemen's sports were covered widely in the press, star firemen were famous, and the musters attracted crowds averaging nearly three thousand. Many other "work-sports" were enormously popular, from laying railroad tracks, lumberjacking, and rock-drilling to office sports such as typesetting and dictation. In 1938, roughly a million spectators attended cornhusking competitions across America, not counting listeners of the live radio broadcasts. Typewriter manufacturers sponsored popular speed typists and large crowds would gather to watch the champions face off.

The analogy to sport helps explain certain corporate strategies. We are so accustomed to executives promoting plans for growth that it would be eccentric to ask: "Why do you need to grow?" It's a rare executive who announces that the firm's business opportunities are dwindling, its competitors are too formidable, and the cost of fighting them is too high, so the plan is to shrink at the right pace. Perhaps growth is a default imperative for businesses because it allows workers to tackle real difficulties. A stagnant firm, no matter how profitable, deprives employees of a key reason to come to work. It's no fun. Even mergers and acquisitions may be gambits to stave off boredom. Given that they rarely raise the share price of the acquiring company, generating fresh challenges may be part of the appeal.[25]

Under the right conditions, workplace victories can be sweet even if they lose money. In the mid-1990s, my boss's boss at the Japanese bank DKB, Mr. Hosaka, visited from the bank's head office in Tokyo. He wanted to win a strategic transaction for an important client. I asked if it was okay to take a loss on the deal. He answered, "We have other ways to make money." I took these instructions as a beautiful frontal attack on the simplistic model of work as an exchange of time and effort for financial compensation. Skeptics may claim that Mr. Hosaka planned to make even more money from the client by giving away a "loss leader." But I know that's not what he meant. He wanted this victory.

Purposeful versus For-Itself

A Peace Treaty

We are now ready to expand the earlier diagram and take one final tour of the main categories of action. Along the way, we'll address the question: What are the benefits of recognizing the boundary between the purposeful and for-itself realms?

In the updated diagram, alternatives to purposeful choice appear in parentheses under each category of for-itself action, while the list on the right describes rationalizations that we use to conceal the importance of for-itself activity from ourselves. When we hew to preestablished beliefs, we concoct reasons to mistrust arguments to the contrary; when we frame an unpredictable altruistic gesture as purposeful, we might explain that "what goes around comes around" or that it will win points with a divine scorekeeper; and, finally, for action over time, we retroactively supply a "reasonable" motive after behaving impulsively.

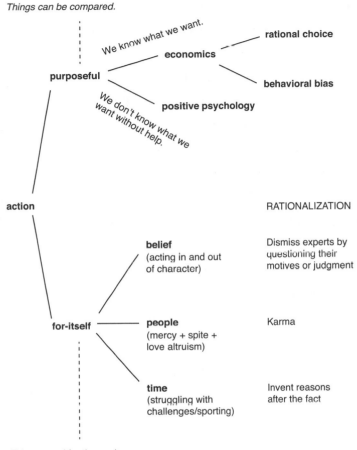

Things can be compared.

We know what we want.

purposeful

economics — rational choice

behavioral bias

We don't know what we want without help. — positive psychology

action

RATIONALIZATION

belief
(acting in and out
of character)

Dismiss experts by
questioning their
motives or judgment

for-itself

people
(mercy + spite +
love altruism)

Karma

time
(struggling with
challenges/sporting)

Invent reasons
after the fact

Things stand for themselves.

Rational Choice

Which makes a better grilled cheese sandwich—Gruyère or cheddar? Gruyère, as far as I'm concerned. Which is better—a Ferris wheel or a roller coaster? Probably a Ferris wheel, but it would depend on the specifics. Which is better—a grilled cheese sandwich or a ride on a Ferris wheel? Well, that's tougher. Out of context, the only sensible answer is, "They're different, you can't compare them." But in our lives we do have to choose. I might settle for suboptimal cheese or skip the sandwich altogether to take my children to an amusement park (sadly, they're too old for that, but you get the idea). If I live a remotely rational life, if I'm optimizing to satisfy my preferences in any meaningful way, I must choose among options that are not commensurable in the narrow sense of two types of cheese or two types of rides. The more difficult which-is-better questions must be answered in order to make the best use of limited resources.

Do I renovate the kitchen or go on a vacation? Do I take the scenic route or hurry home to watch TV? Comparisons, whether complicated or simple, lie at the heart of the rational choice model. Before we can act, we must assign values to each option based on our preferences and how much we already have. Optimization requires that the utility we derive from the last dollar spent on each good or service is the same as the utility of the last dollar spent on every other good or service. If it weren't, we could do better by redirecting our dollars to the good or service that generates more satisfaction on the margin.

Money, though closely associated with the rational choice model, is not essential to this calculation. The question "how much would you pay for one more apple?" could instead be posed as "what fraction of an hour would you be willing to work for one more apple?" Same question, but in the second formulation we divide every price by an hourly wage. Without changing the analysis, we could express every trade-off in terms of hours worked or consumable goods. We speak in terms of money as a matter of convenience, but the same logic would apply to a barter economy.

I suspect that those with a visceral dislike of economics or the quantitative social sciences are reacting to this abstraction and to the premise of commensurability more broadly. Likewise, antipathy toward an excessive concern with money may at heart be uneasiness over the calculations that the use of money implies. Perhaps those who snipe at economics—arguing that it's defective because it failed to predict the most recent economic crisis— are really rebelling against the whole enterprise. They may object to the way rational choice squeezes all our options into a common metric or the way a singular focus on rational choice obscures our ability to see the for-itself side of life.

Whether cast in monetary or other terms, rational choice relates closely to the idea that people can quantify the strength of each desire on a common scale. If you think that sounds mechanistic, then consider Jeremy Bentham's burlesque version of this idea. In the late eighteenth century, Bentham devised an algorithm for estimating the pleasure or pain that would result from any decision. His "felicific calculus" combines fourteen basic pleasures, including expectation, wealth, skill, and amity, as well as twelve basic pains, and adjusts for factors like the intensity and duration of each variable. Any of the twenty-six basic inputs can be traded for another to maximize well-being subject to the prevailing constraints.[1]

In Bentham's utilitarianism, each person is born in the straitjacket of the felicific calculus and can never escape.[2] Although tastes may vary, there is a single correct course of action in every situation—one need only do the math. (To be fair, Bentham was mainly interested in social reform. He didn't encourage individuals to work through the felicific calculus when making life decisions. Nevertheless, Bentham's utilitarianism leaves his followers with a sterile conception of human agency.)

Rational choice does at least allow for unlimited variation among individual preferences and some scope to shape those preferences over a lifetime. But the difference between rational choice when it's applied to decision-making and Bentham's utilitarianism is one of degree rather than kind. In both cases, choice becomes a passive calculation.

Rational choice, then, reduces what people want to one word: more. This "more" is one-dimensional because everything is commensurable, everything can be compared and evaluated. In this view, a failure to attain "more" results strictly from bad luck or bad decisions.

Behavioral Bias

Purposeful choice's explanation for non-maximizing action is behavioral economics. This field investigates the systematic mistakes that we could correct by recognizing our biases and mental shortcuts.

It shouldn't be hard to persuade anyone who falls for the *gambler's fallacy* that the ball is no more likely to land on red in the next spin of the roulette wheel because it was red the last five times or the opposite, that black is not due to catch up.

A person exhibiting *loss aversion* might reject a bet with a 50 percent chance of winning two dollars and a 50 percent chance of losing one dollar. She pays over the odds to avoid small losses because losing is accompanied by psychological discomfort. (This is different from risk aversion, which deals with losses on a large scale.) This bias had better be contained if you're in the business of taking financial risks.

After an event transpires, you may feel that you saw it coming, that you knew it all along, even though you didn't. Behavioral economists call this the *hindsight effect.* This bias is pernicious, since perceiving outcomes as inevitable makes it harder to learn from experience.

It's not always easy to distinguish among behavioral bias, rational choice, and for-itself behavior.

Biases That Are Mostly Rational Choice

Sometimes a phenomenon classified as a behavioral bias is really rational choice in disguise. For instance, given that the chances of winning are incredibly remote, the sale of lottery tickets gets blamed on the *optimism bias* or simply a *bias toward overestimating small probabilities* (twin to the bias toward treating small probabilities as if they were zero). But we don't have to resort to cognitive biases to explain the lottery. Perhaps people buy lottery tickets to animate fantasies of wealth that will wipe their cares away. As Aristotle reminds us, "It is pleasant for [a person] to think he will get what he wants; but no one wants things that seem impossible for himself to attain."[3] Buying the ticket converts the dream of getting rich quick from impossible to possible, and some people must find that appealing.

Biases That Are Mostly For-Itself

The difficulty of recognizing for-itself actions makes them particularly prone to misclassification as behavioral biases. As we saw in Part 2, confidence in one's own opinions is central to holding on to an identity. We tend to believe in ourselves. While this may look to an observer like a failure to optimize, it stands apart from purposeful concerns. If we miss this distinction, however, we might mistake a behavior that is both natural and necessary for overconfidence from the *optimistic bias*, which has been called "the most significant of the cognitive biases."[4] Or we might diagnose it as *confirmation bias*, a tendency to notice and remember information that confirms what we already believe.

The *omission bias* refers to a tendency to favor inaction in decisions with moral consequences. Many people who would be unlikely to push the fat man in the trolley problem would be even less likely to catch him if he slipped on a banana peel and was about to fall onto the tracks and save five people. Either way, as we saw in Chapter 7, this choice is for-itself. It only looks like a bias if we assume that any concern for others has to be care altruism inside a utility function.

Similarly, if we insist on seeing all behavior as purposeful, we might attribute the difficulty of staying with a plan over time to *hyperbolic discounting*. Today, we prefer one consumption stream; tomorrow another. We'd even pay to get out of the plan we'd selected. But as discussed in Chapter 8 and the Online Technical Appendix (www.willful-appendix.com), this is not a behavioral bias; rather, choosing through time belongs to the for-itself realm.

Positive Psychology

The final branch of purposeful behavior in our diagram is positive psychology, or happiness research. This field assumes that studying what appears to satisfy others can teach us about our own natures. Implicit to this project is the assumption that self-reported happiness corresponds to something real. But when asked, "Are you happy?" it's natural to wonder, "Compared to what?" I can report my well-being relative to either how I used to feel or how I imagine people around me feel. Thus the major empirical findings of happiness research are unsurprising: reported happiness is more a function of the rate of income growth (habituation) and relative income (rivalry) than the income level itself.[5]

This field has recently emphasized the importance of "flow"

for enhancing self-reported well-being. As Martin Seligman says, it's about "being one with the music."[6] To get more flow, Seligman, who plays bridge in the upper echelon, recommends picking challenges that correspond to your greatest talents (if he's to be believed, then I should give up trying to learn Japanese).

Seligman's "flow" has elements in common with the for-itself realm: overcoming obstacles and emphasizing gameplay over utility maximization. Seligman goes further, though, by creating a quantitative measure of well-being. And while he doesn't take that measure too literally or stray too far into Bentham territory, he does incorporate flow, or "engagement," as an input into well-being. This creates a contradiction: when you're at one with the music, you can't also be evaluating, comparing, or optimizing. As we've seen, it's a circle that Seligman will never fully square. Flow/engagement can't be quantified and maximized as part of a larger formula.

For-Itself

The for-itself realm encompasses surprising or spontaneous actions, such as a wild leap out of character, a struggle to overcome a challenge that has been freely chosen, and a fierce adherence to an opinion after the time is long past to give it up. Exercising one's will on the world is the key to this realm.

The urge to place all behavior in the purposeful realm can be hard to resist. If people like adventure, sensation, challenges, and overcoming obstacles, why not just plug them into the traditional rational choice framework? Couldn't a rational agent assign a low utility to overcoming challenges if the probability of success were too close to either 0 percent or 100 percent? If people like to act in character, treat themselves to an occasional altruistic gesture and so on, why not put a price on it? Agents would then be able to solve the resulting maximization problem, and rational choice seems like it should do just fine.[7]

But, as we have seen, this can't be done. Some options are wholly incommensurable and inhabit the for-itself realm. Three major categories of action—acting within our identity, engaging in certain altruistic gestures (mercy and love altruism), and organizing ourselves through time—are unlike the choice between cheese versus cheese or even cheese versus Ferris wheel; they just don't fit into an optimization problem.

I have developed various arguments in this book to show that purposeful choice cannot explain all action. Just assessing potential new beliefs triggers "the irritation of doubt," so we stick with what we think we know. Adoption of identity-stretching beliefs leads to new preferences and, in the absence of a homunculus to direct the formation of potential identities, there's no clear way to optimize. We also saw that certain altruistic gestures—but not all—are spontaneous and unpredictable. Others are bigger than the purposeful choice apparatus. Finally, we showed mathematically that it's impossible to have preferences about different arrangements of consumption through time unless we make strange, implausible assumptions. At heart, all these arguments share a common intuition: acts of will can't arise out of passive calculations to satisfy preferences or they would no longer be acts of will.

A last-ditch defense of the theory that all behavior is purposeful might be: "So what? It's only a model; it was never supposed to be a perfect description of the world." But I don't find that persuasive. As we've seen, the purposeful model falls short in important areas of life. Nor would I be persuaded by the argument that classifying action as for-itself means giving up on understanding it. Granted, it's hard to see how for-itself action could be modeled with the rigor of rational choice. Unlike mathematics, which deals with the general, the for-itself concerns particulars, making it difficult to abstract. But a for-itself analysis of action has provided insight into many practical matters.

Just Because

We can benefit in several ways from understanding the boundary between the two realms. "Benefit" is perhaps an odd word when we're talking about the for-itself, but it's fair to ask what we can get out of all this. First, it can help us become more productive in the old-fashioned sense. We have already discussed ways in which seeing where the purposeful ends and the for-itself begins can make us better economists, investors, business managers, philanthropists, or policymakers. Second, recognizing the difference allows us to feel more at ease with behavior that we might otherwise be tempted to pathologize, yet it still leaves room for improvement through studying biases and heuristics. Finally it can mitigate a sense of fragmentation in our lives. Each of these concerns, even the last two, is a benefit in the rational choice realm; when I consult my inventory of desires, I'll surely find being more at ease with my foibles and reduced alienation to be among them. If push came to shove, I suppose I could tell you how much alienation I'd accept on the margin in exchange for a slightly bigger kitchen.

To revisit an example from Chapter 4, institutional investors who recognize the distinction between the purposeful and the for-itself will make more money. They'll relax their reflexive commitment to the "best practices" of the purposeful realm: metrics, market efficiency, mathematical models, attributing expected returns to various risk factors, and analysis based on measures of risk and reward. Instead, they'll accept that real opportunities are unique. Each one stands for itself. Individuals who have "on the spot" knowledge that cannot be fully transmitted to others need to be able to act. This was what David Ricardo did when he bought British government bonds on the eve of Waterloo, and what many other successful investors have done before and since. How can an institution take similar for-itself leaps without descending into recklessness? This, too, comes down to the specifics. There is, and there can be, no general answer.

Beyond improving our results as we seek to gratify desires, acknowledging the for-itself gives us license to embrace specific conduct that we can't credibly explain to ourselves or others in terms of purposeful choice. Keep working beyond the point when you can afford to retire. Don't let the logic of rational choice bully you into hiring a gardener if you like mowing your own grass. Hold onto your beliefs, argue with those who oppose you—you can stand your ground without feeling that you're debating in bad faith. As the trolley approaches, push or don't push the fat man—it's up to you. Hold open the subway door for a stranger even though you know it does more collective harm than good. You don't need a rationalization for an inefficient altruistic gesture any more than the Good Samaritan did when he showered all that attention on one random man. Answering "just because" can be good enough.

Accepting the coexistence of the two realms is a therapy for those of us who are steeped in the theory of rational choice and feel disoriented when we try to reconcile our actions with its monolithic vision. Throughout this book, I've offered examples of individuals trying and failing to integrate abstracted versions of themselves or to make sense of their choices in terms of rationality. In the discussion of choice through time, a person applying the rational model had to referee an unwinnable fight between her present and future selves. Similarly, someone contemplating decisions that would change her beliefs risked becoming a new person with new preferences; adopting the language of fragmentation, she "debated with herself." Stuck in this mode of thinking, she had to imagine the potential new identity that would result from each course of action, then assign the final decision to a homunculus who saw the whole scene from an even more detached point of view. Accepting the dual character of our actions, as depicted in the schema at the beginning of this chapter, can form the basis for a peace treaty between these warring selves.

The study of economics, which is now widespread even in high schools, transmits the alienation that comes from seeing the world in terms of abstract agents who calculate on behalf of potential selves. Economics students learn to think of themselves and others as agents that rationally optimize fixed preferences subject to constraints. By studying game theory, they come to view their opponents as agents seeking their own advantage and to understand that their opponents see them the same way. Studies have shown that those who study economics are less cooperative in games like the ultimatum game, but that's another point altogether.[8]

Whether or not they make students selfish, such habits of thought are clearly conducive to a mechanistic understanding of life. Knowledge becomes nothing more than an instrument for maneuvering through the world. The reduction of all motives to a single abstraction takes us as far as possible from the concrete, unique individual. Rational choice economics can untether us from life as it is lived.

This is not to say that we should abandon the study of economic theory, but that it may be wise to reflect on its perils. Now, when I teach economics, I'm careful to address the for-itself realm. By recognizing that our thought process is not broken if we can't explain "why," perhaps we can protect ourselves from the consequences of overexposure. Perhaps teachers of economics (including me) ought to know when it's time to "leave them kids alone."

But "them kids" should still learn their economics. A million insights, large and small, come from seeing the world in terms of agents with stable preferences doing their best. Why do people in Houston keep their homes cooler in January than those living in Toronto? The answer, according to rational choice: it's optimal to invest in thicker walls and more efficient heaters in colder climates, so the extra cost of raising the temperature when it's cold outside is lower in Toronto. Why does an increase in wages generally reduce the amount of crime? Rational choice sees crime as just another occupation; as opportunities in the non-crime sector improve, the least-satisfied criminals raise their utility by going straight.

Nobody has to go all the way, though, as I once did, in clinging to the belief that rational choice explains everything. Life is complicated, and why shouldn't it be? Not only does recognizing the for-itself realm improve our understanding of practical matters, it also facilitates a closer, more organic connection to our own choices.

Notes

ONE

Venturing beyond Purposeful Choice

1. Schopenhauer, *World as Will and Idea*, 1:29.
2. Williams, "Persons, Character and Morality," 18.
3. See Loewenstein, "The Weighting of Waiting."
4. Keynes, "My Early Beliefs," 96.
5. These ideas can be found in David Hume's *Treatise of Human Nature*, in which he said: "Reason is, and ought only to be the slave of the passions, and can never pretend to any other office than to serve and obey them" (415). They appear again in Arthur Schopenhauer's *The World as Will and Idea* and *On the Fourfold Root of the Principle of Sufficient Reason*, and in Friedrich Nietzsche's *Will to Power*, where he wrote, "Everything of which we become conscious is a terminal phenomenon, an end—and causes nothing . . . And we have sought to understand the world through the reverse conception" (265).
6. Dostoevsky, *Notes from Underground*, 21.
7. Ibid., 25.
8. Nietzsche, *Philosophy in the Tragic Age*, 54–55.

TWO

Two Realms of Human Behavior

1. Kierkegaard, *Either/Or*, 163–164.
2. Becker, *Economic Approach*, 5. Neoclassical economics could be challenged on the assumption of perfect exchange, i.e., markets in equilibrium, and many have done so. Trading may break down due to heterogeneous goods and information asymmetries, imperfect performance on contracts, prices set via strategic bargaining rather than a Walrasian auctioneer, sheer deceit—you name it. In this case, observed behavior will fail to conform to neoclassical models and economists' policy prescriptions will not fit the real world. See, e.g., Kohn, "Value and Exchange." But that is not our focus. Here we are concerned with motives at the level of the individual.
3. Thaler, "Consumer Choice," 43–47.
4. This logic resembles that of theorems on the impossibility of voting schemes that fully reflect social preferences. See, e.g., Arrow, *Social Choice*, 46–60.
5. Simon, "Rational Choice."
6. Nietzsche, *Thus Spoke Zarathustra*, 33–35.
7. Hsee et al., "Overearning," 852–853.
8. Richtel, "Can't Take It with You."

THREE

Acting in Character

1. Whitman, "Song of Myself."
2. In "Economics and Identity," Akerlof and Kranton model identity in terms of rational choice theory. In their setup, each person is assigned to an identity group, such as gender, with corresponding tastes for different types of action. An individual's utility function includes conforming to the assigned identity (failure to do so imposes an unpleasant drop in identity) and a preference that others who share the same identity perform the prescribed actions. Violators or "mavericks" lessen group cohesion. One might seek to rein in mavericks by threatening to punish them with ridicule or ostracism. This imposes a cost on the punishers as well as the punished, so punishment is worthwhile to the extent that the cost to the punishers is low, their concern for group conformity is high, and potential mavericks are easily deterred. This model can account for workplace discrimination, social exclusion, sorting by gender into occupations, and certain aspects of allocation of time in the household if, for instance, a wife preferred to act in accordance with traditional roles. The authors note that rules can evolve,

and indeed after less than twenty years, their examples, like secretaries who are called "office wives" to male bosses, feel straight out of a time capsule. Rereading Akerlof and Kranton today, one is struck by the fruits of social progress: looser rules and reduced pressure to conform. I am using "identity" in a much broader sense than Akerlof and Kranton, to refer to the totality of an individual's attitudes and beliefs. This sense of "identity" can accommodate, for example, rebellion against gender roles. More importantly, it includes behavior that does not stem from membership in any particular group, such as a person subscribing to alternative medicine even if others in her Akerlof-and-Kranton-assigned identity group do not.

3. Peirce, "Fixation of Belief."
4. Kierkegaard, *Fear and Trembling/Repetition*, 132–133.
5. There is no direct evidence linking this famous quote to Keynes, although Joan Robinson wrote in the *Economic Journal* in 1986 that Keynes would say it whenever he was accused of being inconsistent. The *Wall Street Journal* quoted Paul Samuelson in 1978 attributing a similar remark to Keynes. For an impressively rigorous analysis of the provenance of this quote, see http://quoteinvestigator.com/2011/07/22/keynes-change-mind/ (accessed February 7, 2019).
6. Nyhan et al., "Effective Messages in Vaccine Promotion," 835.
7. Twain, *Tom Sawyer Abroad*, 77.
8. Hayek, "Use of Knowledge."
9. The Supreme Court of the United Kingdom, Judgment in the matter of Lehman Brothers International (Europe) (in Administration) and in the Matter of the Insolvency Act 1986 (February 29, 2012), full transcript at https://www.supremecourt.uk/cases/docs/uksc-2010-0194-judgment.pdf (accessed February 7, 2019).
10. Russell, *Problems of Philosophy*, 96.
11. Darwin, *Life and Letters*, 310.
12. Kierkegaard, *Fear and Trembling/Repetition*, 43. Whatever his flaws, John D. Rockefeller was a knight of faith. In March 1930, during some of the darkest days of the Great Depression, he broke ground on New York City's Rockefeller Center. He later said, "It was clear that there were only two courses open to me. One was to abandon the entire development. The other was to go forward with it in the definite knowledge that I myself would have to build it and finance it alone" (Okrent, *Great Fortune*, 70). "I," "myself," and "alone." Rockefeller could have made more money with less risk by buying a diversified portfolio of shares, but he was already rich, and that's not what he wanted to do. Two other knights of faith, John Jakob Raskob and Al Smith, reportedly hatched a plan to build the world's tallest building in November 1928 to revive their spirits after Smith lost the presidency to Herbert Hoover. They announced the Empire State Building on August 29, 1929.

Smith and Raskob raised money while the stock market crashed, broke ground on Saint Patrick's Day in March 1930, and opened on May 1, 1931 (Berman, *Empire State Building*, 11).

FOUR

Making Money in Financial Markets

1. Stalwart believers in efficient markets will even deny the existence of market "bubbles." In at least some cases, they're right. For instance, most people believe that seventeenth-century Dutch traders lost their minds, bidding up the price of tulips to incredible heights and causing an economic crisis when prices finally collapsed. According to Peter Garber's 1989 article debunking tulipmania, modern references to the tulip craze are based on a brief description from 1852 that drew in turn on unreliable secondary sources. Garber's investigation shows that the price of rare bulbs did soar from 1634 to 1637, then gradually fell. But a temporary spike in prices for rare bulbs was a normal phenomenon for tulips as it was for hyacinths. A rare bulb could be propagated by asexual reproduction to double the supply each year, so a buyer could recover the initial outlay by selling off the new supply as prices declined. The only real oddity is the wild rise in the price of common bulbs in January 1637 before they plummeted that February. This spike appears to be the result of bets made in bars by traders goofing around—they put no money behind the contracts, had no money to pay, and perhaps no expectation that the contracts would be enforced. There are no credible contemporaneous accounts of economic distress; the speculation caused only the transfer of wealth, and little wealth was transferred in the end.

2. Zeckhauser, "Investing in the Unknown and Unknowable." Ricardo persuaded Thomas Malthus to join him in buying bonds, but Malthus chickened out before the battle and sold at a small profit.

3. Smith, *Wealth of Nations*, 64. Emphasis mine.

FIVE

For-Itself Decision-Making within a Group

1. Even if the entrepreneur did manage to convince the venture capitalist, many communication hurdles would still lie ahead. The information that must be communicated is at its most intimate, unique, and personal at the start of a firm's life. For this reason, initial funding for startups usually comes from those with the best chance of connecting with the entrepre-

neur's vision—family and close friends. Next come "angel investors," rich individuals who invest their own money. Often, the angel already knows the entrepreneur. After the business has gone a certain distance, it is ready for venture capital. The entrepreneur can expect a personal relationship, up to a point, with venture capitalists who are prepared to take the leap. But if the goal is a public offering of stock, the company must make a mountain of information available as freely transmittable facts. Privacy and close personal relationships are replaced by the larger investment community and the impersonal contact between managers and public investors. When a deal expands from a close personal circle to include the general public, communicating beliefs becomes quantumly more difficult.

SIX
Altruism

1. In business, cooperative behavior can be beneficial in two ways. First, it's impossible to draw up contracts that anticipate every possible contingency. Even if it were possible, contracts would still be costly to monitor and enforce. A party with a reputation for fair dealing can be counted on to stick to the spirit of a written or unwritten agreement even when he is not legally obligated to do so. Second, repeat dealings can facilitate gains from efficient favors when the transfer of money is prohibited by law or social convention. Today, I'll scratch your back if it benefits you by more than it costs me. In the future, the opportunity might arise for you to scratch mine. But we have to trust each other.

2. Roth et al., "Bargaining and Market Behavior." In a multiplayer version of the game, the allocators kept almost everything and the receivers accepted small offers. This held up in all four cities and became particularly pronounced after several rounds as players learned. Norms evidently do not apply in the same way when the opponent is a crowd rather than an individual.

3. Andersen et al., "Stakes Matter." Like manners, the social norms for fairness and punishing unfairness vary across societies. Studies by Henrich et al. ("Markets, Religion," and "Costly Punishment") have shown that allocators offer larger shares of the pot in societies that are integrated with markets (e.g., wage workers in Accra City, Ghana, versus nomadic foragers in the savanna woodlands of Tanzania). For example, allocators among the Tsimane, hunter-gatherers in the jungles of Bolivia, offered an average of only 26 percent of the pot. The lower the offer, the more frequently it was rejected in all fifteen societies studied, although rejection rates differed sharply across societies. Most notably, members of small communities and

those lacking market economies are more likely to accept low offers. For instance, 85 percent of inhabitants of Yasawa Island, Fiji (engaged in horticulture and marine foraging) accepted offers as low as 10 percent of the pot, while 100 percent of Emory University freshmen and Gusii (mixed farming/wage workers in the high plains of Kenya) rejected all offers of less than 40 percent. Evidently, societies less experienced with anonymous market transactions had not yet developed sophisticated norms for fairness in this kind of commerce, so players went for the highest payoff.

4. Becker, "Theory of Social Interactions," 1074–1083. See the Online Technical Appendix (www.willful-appendix.com) for a simple example illustrating the Rotten Kid Theorem.

5. Singer, "Drowning Child."

6. As Larissa MacFarquhar describes in *Strangers Drowning: Voyages to the Brink of Moral Extremity*, extreme effective altruists give kidneys to strangers. One of the book's subjects was racked with guilt over buying a candy apple rather than using the four dollars for a malaria net to send to Africa. Extreme effective altruists do not promote Rawlsian justice, exactly, and seek to help the absolute worst off, although those in deep poverty are ripe targets for aid. Another of the book's subjects, Aaron, refused to pay off the credit-card debt of a homeless former girlfriend because starving people in the developing world needed the money more. Extreme effective altruists only sleep or relax to restore energy so they can earn more money to donate; Aaron optimized his motions, placing his computer in his bedroom so "he could roll out of bed and push the on button with one movement" (54). It reached the point that "everything Aaron bought, even the smallest cheapest thing, felt to him like food or medicine snatched from someone dying" (44).

7. Smith, *Theory of Moral Sentiments*, 1–2.

8. In terms of an optimization problem, this is technically a "corner solution." I give zero. Abstracting from feelings of guilt, a Yankees fan who gives nothing would theoretically take money away from the team if he could do so without getting caught. The exception would be the knife-edge condition, where care is just about to rise to the surface. In this case, an individual who gives nothing but is indifferent to giving one dollar would not take money from the cause if given the chance.

9. A simple numerical example will clarify this point. Suppose Consumer #1 cares about both Consumer #2 and Consumer #3, who in turn care about only their own consumption. The following formula describes Consumer #1's utility, which depends on the consumption of all three:

$$\text{Utility of Consumer \#1} = U(c_1, c_2, c_3) =$$
$$ln(c_1) + 0.75 \, ln(4 + \Delta c_2) + 0.5 \, ln(14.2 + \Delta c_3).$$

This formula tells us that #2 starts out poorer than #3, with 4 units versus 14.2. $4 + \Delta c_2$ is #2's consumption, which she obtains from her 4-unit endowment plus Δc_2 transferred from #1. $14.2 + \Delta c_3$ is #3's consumption, which she gets from her 14.2-unit endowment and a transfer of Δc_3 from #1. The term $ln(4 + \Delta c_2)$ is the utility of #2 as she experiences it, $ln(14.2 + \Delta c_3)$ is the utility of #3, and $ln(c_1)$ is the utility that #1 derives from her own consumption.

Because #1 weights #2's consumption by 0.75, she must care less about #2's consumption than her own. She cares about #3's consumption even less, weighting it at 0.5. This does not make #1 selfish: although she privileges her own consumption, her care for both of the others is genuine and reasonably strong.

#1 maximizes her utility subject to her budget constraint. Assuming her income is 10, then her budget is:

$$c_1 + \Delta c_2 + \Delta c_3 = 10.$$

Both transfers must be nonnegative, i.e., #1 can't take money away from #2 or #3 to produce a preferable result:

$$\Delta c_2 \geq 0,$$
$$\Delta c_3 \geq 0.$$

If #1 maximized her utility while ignoring the constraints that $\Delta c_2 \geq 0$ and $\Delta c_3 \geq 0$, she would simply equate the marginal utility of her own consumption to the (weighted) marginal utility of #2 and #3. Given our numerical assumptions, she would want to transfer consumption away from #3 to both herself and #2. That's because #3 is so rich, the marginal benefit of #3's consumption (from #1's perspective) is small, particularly considering that #3's welfare has a 0.5 weighting.

Thus #1 must impose the constraint $\Delta c_3 - 0$. Her solution is $c_1^* = 8$ and $\Delta c_2^* = 2$. That is, #1 achieves the greatest utility by transferring 2 units to #2, transferring nothing to #3 and consuming the remaining 8 out of her budget. In this example, #1 cares about #3, just not enough to do anything about it in light of #3's wealth.

But now suppose every \$1 that #1 transferred to #3 would produce a \$4 increase in #3's consumption (perhaps #1 has an asset that #3 values more than she does). In this case, #1's utility takes the following form: $ln(c_1) + 0.75 \, ln(4 + \Delta c_2) + 0.5 \, ln(14.2 + 4 \times \Delta c_3)$.

Maximizing this expression subject to #1's budget, the new solution is $c_1^* = 7.8$, $\Delta c_2^* = 1.85$ and $\Delta c_3^* = 0.35$. The care that #1 has always felt for #3 can now be observed. Transferring to #3 now raises the utility of #1, even though #3 is richer than everyone else and #1 discounts #3's welfare by a factor of 2.

Everything discussed in this endnote is care altruism, perfectly consistent with rational choice.

10. Montaigne, "Taste of Good and Evil," 43.
11. See Andreoni, "Giving with Impure Altruism."
12. Busboom, "Bat 21," 30.
13. De Waal, Leimgruber, and Greenberg, "Giving Is Self-Rewarding," 13685–13687. The authors controlled for various biases, such as whether the monkeys favored their left or right hand. The token exchange was hidden from the monkeys' groups to control for the possibility that the subject would choose the prosocial token out of fear that selfish behavior would be punished after the experiment.
14. We've said that altruism has to impose a cost on the altruist. This example satisfies the definition (barely) because the subject monkeys had to go to the trouble of figuring out which token was which and exerting the energy to make the prosocial choice. The subject monkeys also had to set aside concerns that any food going to the partner monkey would eventually come out of their allocation.
15. The couple run an inefficient household, leaving opportunities on the table to make both better off. While an inefficient household proves that they don't exhibit care altruism, an efficient household would not be sufficient to prove that they did. For instance, they may not care at all about each other but be very good at coordinating. The husband might then walk the dog so the wife can work late and contribute the extra money to joint expenditures that benefit the husband. To distinguish care altruism from effective coordination, we'd have to consider a case where one spouse was unaware that the other had advanced his interests.
16. Bentham, *Introduction to the Principles of Morals and Legislation*, 36.
17. Sartre, *Existentialism Is a Humanism*, 30–31.

SEVEN

Public Policy

1. This is not the textbook normative versus positive distinction. I assume the policymaker knows everyone's preferences, including values—e.g., environmental standards, income equality, equality of opportunity, and so forth. With all this information, the policymaker can factor values into the pursuit of Pareto efficiency.
2. Taylor, *Rationality*, 20. Taylor's aim is to "overthrow" economic theory by identifying examples with no Pareto-efficient solution. He starts his book with several such stories of people refusing to give something up for money. Taylor, however, is launching his assault on a straw man. He has not proven that the rational choice model is useless—simply that it does not apply to every decision.

3. Cicero, *De Officiis*, 319–325; Foot, "Problem of Abortion," 23.
4. Cicero, *De Officiis*, 321.
5. To the extent that some people are hungrier than others, the distribution of income is unequal, Rhodes lacks a "social safety net" that ensures minimal grain allotments to the poor, and the wait before the next ships arrive is substantial, the allocation of grain will deviate from the social optimum if the merchant fails to disclose. If everyone knew that more grain was coming, some richer, less-hungry people would wait to make their purchase, thereby driving prices down before the next ships arrive and allowing poorer, hungrier people to eat sooner.
6. Thomson, "Trolley Problem," 1397–1399.
7. If we can truly exclude the possibility of the questioner cheating, however, then odds of 1 in a trillion for $0.25 should appeal to many people. Playing 10 million times, you'd have about a 1 in 100,000 chance of death in exchange for $2.5 million. To put this in context, assume a person can expect to live another 50 years. The expected loss of life from betting with 1 in 100,000 odds of losing is 262 minutes. Assuming each cigarette cuts 10 minutes from a person's life, this wager would correspond to a smoker skipping 26 cigarettes for $2.5 million. If the bet feels too risky to you, make the odds 1 in 10 trillion. If you still resist, I suspect that you just don't trust the questioner to play fairly, no matter what anyone says.
8. Searle, "Philosophy of Society, Lecture 20," 41:00–58:00.

EIGHT
Changing Our Minds

1. For a formal statement and proof of this proposition, see my 2009 paper "Nietzsche and the Economics of Becoming," and for a more general, upgraded proof, see the Online Technical Appendix (www.willful-appendix .com). In a very similar setup to "Nietzsche and the Economics of Becoming," Simone Galperti and Bruno Strulovici independently prove the same result: "an agent who cares about his well-being beyond the immediate future [i.e., more than one period ahead] cannot be time consistent" ("From Anticipations to Present Bias," 9; see also "Forward-Looking Behavior Revisited," 13). This means a person who looks ahead more than one period will inevitably change his mind. In a 2017 follow-up, Galperti and Strulovici apply the theorem to intergenerational transfers, replacing future selves with future generations linked by altruism. The Online Technical Appendix shows how the notation and assumptions of Galperti and Strulovici map onto my own.
2. Of course, the agent could maximize given perfect knowledge of how

he'll behave in the future, because any function can be maximized given regularity conditions. In the first period the agent chooses what is best, anticipating what he'll freely choose in the next period. The resulting consumption plan will differ, however, from the optimal plan assuming control over the future. See the Online Technical Appendix (www.willful -appendix.com) for details. A certain stability also arises in models where the individual is made up of subagents, or homunculi, who enter into dynamic bargaining games and can undertake actions on the individual's behalf. The one with the long-term interest will punish the one with the short-term interest if it causes the individual to indulge too much or too often. "Wasteful" procrastination can emerge from the bargaining. But even as the subagent tried to optimize its own preferences, it would still be subject to the limits on time-consistent preferences. See Ross, "Economic Models of Procrastination," for a summary.

3. To express these steps mathematically, define h_t as the hedonic index that measures a person's well-being at time t:

$$h_t = U(c_t) + \frac{h_{t+1}}{1 + \rho}.$$

Well-being today depends on the utility derived from current-period consumption, $U(c_t)$, and the discounted value of the next period's well-being. Repeated substitution leads to a representation of the agent's objective that is familiar to economists:

$$\max \sum_{t=1}^{n} \frac{U(c_t)}{(1 + \rho)^{t-1}} \text{ subject to budget constraint}$$

where n = number of periods.

The solution that maximizes h_t in the earlier expression is time consistent, so an optimal path from the perspective of $t = 1$ will remain optimal as future periods arrive. It works for an infinite period as long as ρ is greater than the interest rate. See the Online Technical Appendix (www.willful -appendix.com) for details.

4. See the Online Technical Appendix (www.willful-appendix.com). Formally, this analysis also applies to intergenerational transfers. It is impossible for the generations of a family to plot a time-consistent course connected by mutual care. But the way generations interact differs fundamentally from an individual confronting her own life in different time periods, so the near impossibility of time consistency is less remarkable.

5. That formula is geometric discounting. See the Online Technical Appendix (www.willful-appendix.com).

6. Someone afflicted with hyperbolic discounting might prefer $50 today to $100 in one year while also preferring $100 in six years to $50 in five years.

When five years have passed, that second preference will reverse, and he'll prefer $50 right away to waiting a year for $100.

7. Gazzaniga, *Ethical Brain*, 148–149.
8. Libet, "Do We Have Free Will?," 49.
9. Nagel, *View from Nowhere*, 127.
10. Schopenhauer, *World as Will and Idea*, 3:118.
11. A 2 percent average annual chance of death in the ancestral environment is consistent with the observation that real interest rates tend to hover around 2 percent; that is, we are compensated by 1 to 2 percent per year above the rate of inflation for waiting.
12. Nozick, *Nature of Rationality*, 14–15.

NINE

Homo Economicus *and* Homo Ludens

1. In 1920, the *Journal of Political Economy* was essentially equation-free (the single equation that year was an accounting identity). By 1930, 15 percent of papers had at least one equation although none with more than high-school-level math. By 1960, the proportion of papers with at least one equation had climbed to 30 percent. It shot up to 90 percent in 1970 and higher math became commonplace.
2. As Jacob Viner wrote in 1925, "There are many who would place greater stress on the importance of the process of desire-fulfillment itself than on the gratifications or other states of consciousness which result from such fulfillment" ("Utility Concept in Value Theory," 641).
3. Veblen, "Limitations of Marginal Utility," 620.
4. Skidelsky, *John Maynard Keynes*, 224.
5. Huizinga, *Homo Ludens*, 13.
6. Keynes, *General Theory of Employment, Interest, and Money*, 160.
7. See Dow and Dow, "Animal Spirits Revisited."
8. Sen, "Maximization," 747.
9. An experimental literature stretching back to 1956 (Brehm, "Postdecision Changes") finds that subjects who choose between two equally valuable options will reevaluate the options after they choose. Subjects tend to increase their assessment of the value of the option they select and decrease their assessment of the value of the one they reject. This is the case even if they choose randomly—a tendency to favor their choice outweighs any "buyer's remorse." But they stop short of upgrading their assessment if a computer picks for them. Somehow they settle into a choice if it results from the free exercise of their will (see Sharot, Velasquez, and Dolan, "Do Decisions Shape Preference?"). While these experiments suggest that con-

sumers care about choosing in itself, I would not go so far as to say that "choices influence preferences." For economics, if not psychology, "preferences" signifies what people actually choose, not how they rate what they've already done.

10. Smith, *Wealth of Nations*, 18.

11. See Delmonico's Dinner Menu, 1899.

12. Iyengar and Lepper, "When Choice Is Demotivating."

13. Tversky and Shafir, "Disjunction Effect," 305–306.

14. Personal finance guides counsel living by a budget, but many people resist this advice. We want each spending decision to feel, to the extent possible, like a unique act of will.

15. Oprea, "Survival versus Profit Maximization," 2227, 2234–2235.

16. Plutarch, *Lives of Illustrious Men*, 438.

17. Ricardo, *On the Principles*, 158–170.

18. Knight, "World Justice, Socialism, and the Intellectuals," 442.

19. See Karabarbounis, "Labor Wedge," 212.

20. Keynes, "Economic Possibilities," 365–373.

21. The grandnephew's comment is from Kestenbaum, "Keynes Predicted."

22. Phelps, *Mass Flourishing*, 19–40; Phelps, "The Good Economy," 6.

23. Nutton, "Seeds of Disease," 11.

24. To understand why these discoveries never exploded into business and commercial activity, we can look to Aristotle, who devalued work aimed at material well-being. Aristotle distinguished between the technical knowledge needed to perform a craft and abstract knowledge, the jurisdiction of philosophers. He argued that since humans alone engage in rational thought, it must be our highest aim. Technical knowledge addresses the needs for food and physical comfort we share with animals. This attitude has proven difficult to shake. As Andrzej Rapaczynski observes, "The Christian and aristocratic worlds provided . . . an incredibly powerful vehicle for carrying the Aristotelian mindset all the way to our times" ("Moral Significance of Economic Life," 5).

25. See, e.g., Alexandridis, Petmezas, and Travlos, "Gains from Mergers and Acquisitions," 1671.

SUMMING UP

Purposeful versus For-Itself

1. Bentham, *Introduction to the Principles of Morals and Legislation*, 29–42.

2. John Stuart Mill was literally born into utilitarianism. Bentham, his father's close friend, trained Mill in his theories from childhood. No wonder Mill had a mental breakdown when he was twenty years old.

3. Aristotle, *On Rhetoric*, 116.
4. Kahneman, *Thinking, Fast and Slow*, 225.
5. I also wonder about the extent to which cross-country happiness data simply measures how people in different cultures respond to surveys. According to the *World Happiness Report 2016* (Helliwell, Layard, and Sachs), Europe's poorest country, Moldova, with GDP per capita of $1,900, a 10 percent population decline since the 2004 census, and an average life expectancy of 67 years, ranked ahead of South Korea (GDP per capita of $28,000). It nearly tied with Italy (GDP per capita of $30,000) and Japan (GDP per capita of $37,000). Moldova, the third-least-visited country in Europe (after Lichtenstein and San Marino, each of which has around 1 percent of Moldova's population and half as many tourists), hosted 120,000 tourists in 2016. This compares with 17 million tourists to South Korea, 52 million to Italy, and 24 million to Japan. Hong Kong, with GDP per capita of $43,000 and 27 million tourists per year, is tied on the happiness scale with Somalia, with GDP per capita of $450 and no tourism (for these data and other comparisons, see worldbank.org, imf.org, and unwto .org). Perhaps people in Japan, South Korea, and Italy are reluctant to boast, while those from repressive regimes or with cultural norms that discourage complaining report that they are happy regardless of their circumstances.
6. Seligman, *Flourish*, 11.
7. See Heckman, "Comment."
8. Wang, Malhotra, and Murnighan, "Economics Education and Greed," 655.

Bibliography

Akerlof, George A., and Rachel E. Kranton. "Economics and Identity." *Quarterly Journal of Economics* 115, no. 3 (2000): 715–753.

Alexandridis, George, Dimitris Petmezas, and Nickolaos G. Travlos. "Gains from Mergers and Acquisitions around the World: New Evidence." *Financial Management* 39, no. 4 (2010): 1671–1695.

Andersen, Steffen, Seda Ertac, Uri Gneezy, Moshe Hoffman, and John A. List. "Stakes Matter in Ultimatum Games." *American Economic Review* 101, no. 7 (2001): 3427–3439.

Andreoni, James. "Giving with Impure Altruism: Applications to Charity and Ricardian Equivalence." *Journal of Political Economy* 97, no. 6 (1989): 1447–1458.

Aristotle. *On Rhetoric*. Translated by George A. Kennedy. New York: Oxford University Press, 2007.

Arrow, Kenneth J. *Social Choice and Individual Values*. New York: J. Wiley/ Chapman & Hall, 1951.

Becker, Gary S. *The Economic Approach to Human Behavior*. Chicago: University of Chicago Press, 1976.

———. "A Theory of Social Interactions." *Journal of Political Economy* 82, no. 6 (1974): 1063–1093.

Bibliography

Bentham, Jeremy. *An Introduction to the Principles of Morals and Legislation.* London: Clarendon Press, 1907.

Berman, John S. *The Empire State Building.* New York: Museum of the City of New York, 2003.

Brehm, Jack W. "Postdecision Changes in the Desirability of Alternatives." *Journal of Abnormal and Social Psychology* 52, no. 3 (1956): 384–389.

Buber, Martin. *Tales of the Hasidim.* Translated by Olga Marx. New York: Schocken Books, 1991.

Busboom, Stanley L. "Bat 21: A Case Study." U.S. Army War College, Carlisle Barracks, PA: 1990. Retrieved from www.dtic.mil/dtic/tr/fulltext/u2/a220660.pdf (accessed February 2, 2019).

Cicero, Marcus Tullius. *De Officiis.* Book 3. Translated by Walter Miller. New York: Macmillan, 1913.

Darwin, Charles. *The Life and Letters of Charles Darwin, Including an Autobiographical Chapter.* Vol. 1. Edited by Francis Darwin. London: John Murray, 1887.

Delmonico's Dinner Menu, 1899. Rare Book Division, New York Public Library, Digital ID 467783. http://digitalcollections.nypl.org/items/510d47db-3724-a3d9-e040-e00a18064a99 (accessed February 2, 2019).

Dostoevsky, Fyodor. *Notes from Underground.* Translated by Richard Pevear and Larissa Volokhonsky. New York: Random House, 1994.

Dow, Alistair, and Sheila C. Dow. "Animal Spirits Revisited." *Capitalism and Society* 6, no. 2 (2011).

Epstein, Julius J., Philip G. Epstein, and Howard Koch. *Casablanca.* Motion picture. Directed by Michael Curtiz. Warner Bros., 1942.

Foot, Philippa. "The Problem of Abortion and the Doctrine of the Double Effect." In Foot, *Virtues and Vices and Other Essays in Moral Philosophy,* 19–32. Oxford, UK: Clarendon Press, 2002.

Galperti, Simone, and Bruno H. Strulovici. "Forward-Looking Behavior Revisited: A Foundation of Time Inconsistency." Working paper, April 2, 2014. https://economics.yale.edu/sites/default/files/bruno_s.pdf (accessed February 2, 2019).

———. "From Anticipations to Present Bias: A Theory of Forward-Looking Preferences." Working paper, October 31, 2014. https://pdfs.semanticscholar.org/36f1/2ace17c4cb86a086902d1ac27e475f8c945d.pdf (accessed February 2, 2019).

———. "A Theory of Intergenerational Altruism." *Econometrica* 85, no. 4 (2017): 1175–1218.

Bibliography

Garber, Peter M. "Tulipmania." *Journal of Political Economy* 97, no. 3 (1989): 535–560.

Gazzaniga, Michael S. *The Ethical Brain: The Science of Our Moral Dilemmas.* New York: Harper Collins, 2005.

Guthrie, A. B., Jr. *Shane.* Motion picture. Directed by George Stevens. Paramount Pictures, 1953.

Hayek, Friedrich A. "The Use of Knowledge in Society." *American Economic Review* 35, no. 4 (1945): 519–530.

Heckman, James J. "Comment on 'Nietzsche and the Economics of Becoming.'" *Capitalism and Society* 4, no. 1 (2009).

Helliwell, John, Richard Layard, and Jeffrey Sachs. *World Happiness Report 2016, Update.* Vol. 1. New York: Sustainable Development Solutions Network, 2016.

Henrich, Joseph, Jean Ensminger, Richard McElreath, Abigail Barr, Clark Barrett, Alexander Bolyanatz, Juan Camilo Cárdenas, Michael Gurven, Edwins Gwako, Natalie Henrich, Carolyn Lesorogol, Frank Marlowe, David Tracer, and John Ziker. "Markets, Religion, Community Size, and the Evolution of Fairness and Punishment." *Science* 327, no. 5972 (2010): 1480–1484.

Henrich, Joseph, Richard McElreath, Abigail Barr, Jean Ensminger, Clark Barrett, Alexander Bolyanatz, Juan Camilo Cárdenas, Michael Gurven, Edwins Gwako, Natalie Henrich, Carolyn Lesorogol, Frank Marlowe, David Tracer, and John Ziker. "Costly Punishment across Human Societies." *Science* 312, no. 5781 (2006): 1767–1770.

Herrnstein Smith, Barbara. *Contingencies of Value: Alternate Perspectives for Critical Theory.* Cambridge, MA: Harvard University Press, 1988.

Homer. *The Odyssey.* Translated by Richmond Lattimore. New York: Harper & Row, 1967.

Hsee, Christopher K., Jiao Zhang, Cindy F. Cai, and Shirley Zhang. "Overearning." *Psychological Science* 24, no. 6 (2013): 852–859.

Huizinga, Johan. *Homo Ludens: A Study of the Play-Element in Culture.* London: Routledge & Kegan Paul, 1949.

Hume, David. *Treatise of Human Nature.* 2nd ed. Vol. 2: *Of the Passions.* Oxford, UK: Clarendon Press, 1896.

Iyengar, Sheena S., and Mark R. Lepper. "When Choice Is Demotivating: Can One Desire Too Much of a Good Thing?" *Journal of Personality and Social Psychology* 79, no. 6 (2000): 995–1006.

Kahneman, Daniel. *Thinking, Fast and Slow.* New York: Farrar, Straus and Giroux, 2011.

Bibliography

Kahneman, Daniel, and Amos Tversky. "Prospect Theory: An Analysis of Decision under Risk." *Econometrica* 47, no. 2 (1979): 263–291.

Karabarbounis, Loukas. "The Labor Wedge: MRS vs. MPN." *Review of Economic Dynamics* 17, no. 2 (2014): 206–223.

Kestenbaum, David. "Keynes Predicted We Would Be Working 15-Hour Weeks. Why Was He So Wrong?" *NPR Planet Money*. Podcast audio, August 13, 2015. http://www.npr.org/2015/08/13/432122637/keynes -predicted-we-would-be-working-15-hour-weeks-why-was-he-so-wrong (accessed February 2, 2019).

Keynes, John Maynard. "Economic Possibilities for our Grandchildren." In Keynes, *Essays in Persuasion*, 358–373. New York: W.W. Norton, 1963.

———. *The General Theory of Employment, Interest, and Money*. New York: Harcourt, 1964.

———. "My Early Beliefs." In *The Bloomsbury Group: A Collection of Memoirs and Commentary*, edited by S. P. Rosenbaum, 82–97. Toronto: University of Toronto Press, Inc., 1995.

Kierkegaard, Søren. *Either/Or: Part II*. Translated by Howard V. Hong and Edna H. Hong. Princeton, NJ: Princeton University Press, 1987.

———. *Fear and Trembling/Repetition*. Translated by Howard V. Hong and Edna H. Hong. Princeton, NJ: Princeton University Press, 1983.

Knight, Frank H. "The Role of Principles in Economics and Politics." *American Economic Review* 41, no. 1 (1951): 1–29.

———. "World Justice, Socialism, and the Intellectuals." *University of Chicago Law Review* 16, no. 3 (1949): 434–443.

Kohn, Meir. "Value and Exchange." *Cato Journal* 24, no. 3 (2004): 303–339.

Libet, Benjamin. "Do We Have Free Will?" *Journal of Consciousness Studies* 6, nos. 8–9 (1999): 47–57.

Loewenstein, George. "The Weighting of Waiting: Response Mode Effects in Intertemporal Choice." Working paper, Center for Decision Research, University of Chicago, 1988.

MacFarquhar, Larissa. *Strangers Drowning: Voyages to the Brink of Moral Extremity*. New York: Penguin, 2015.

Marshall, Alfred. *Principles of Economics*. London: Macmillan, 1890.

de Montaigne, Michel. "That the Taste of Good and Evil Depends in Large Part on the Opinion We Have of It." In *The Complete Essays of Montaigne*, translated by Donald M. Frame, 33–46. Stanford, CA: Stanford University Press, 1957.

Bibliography

Nagel, Thomas. *The View from Nowhere*. New York: Oxford University Press, 1986.

Nietzsche, Friedrich. *Philosophy in the Tragic Age of the Greeks*. Translated by Marianne Cowan. Chicago: Regnery Publishing, 1962.

———. *Thus Spoke Zarathustra: A Book for Everybody and Nobody*. Translated by Graham Parkes. Oxford, UK: Oxford University Press, 2005.

———. *The Will to Power*. Translated by Walter Kaufmann and R. J. Hollingdale. New York: Vintage, 1967.

Nozick, Robert. *The Nature of Rationality*. Princeton, NJ: Princeton University Press, 1993.

Nutton, Vivian. "The Seeds of Disease: An Explanation of Contagion and Infection from the Greeks to the Renaissance." *Medical History* 27, no. 1 (1983): 1–34.

Nyhan, Brendan, Jason Reifler, Sean Richey, and Gary L. Freed. "Effective Messages in Vaccine Promotion: A Randomized Trial." *Pediatrics* 133, no. 4 (2014): 835–842.

Okrent, Daniel. *Great Fortune: The Epic of Rockefeller Center*. New York: Penguin, 2004.

Online Technical Appendix. https://www.willful-appendix.com.

Oprea, Ryan. "Survival versus Profit Maximization in a Dynamic Stochastic Experiment." *Econometrica* 82, no. 6 (2014): 2225–2255.

Peirce, Charles Sanders. "The Fixation of Belief." *Popular Science Monthly* 12 (1877): 1–15.

Phelps, Edmund S. "The Good Economy: The Vitalism of Aristotle, Cervantes and Bergson and the Economic Justice of Kant and Rawls." Speech, Buenos Aires, May 28, 2007. https://www.researchgate.net /publication/242166276_The_Good_Economy_The_Vitalism_of _Aristotle_Cervantes_and_Bergson_And_the_Economic_Justice_of _Kant_and_Rawls (accessed February 21, 2019).

———. *Mass Flourishing: How Grassroots Innovation Created Jobs, Challenge, and Change*. Princeton, NJ: Princeton University Press, 2013.

Plutarch. *Plutarch's Lives of Illustrious Men*. Vol. 2. Translated by John Dryden. New York: John W. Lovell, 1880.

Poe, Edgar Allan. "The Cask of Amontillado." *Godey's Lady's Book* 33, no. 5 (1846): 216–218.

Rapaczynski, Andrzej. "The Moral Significance of Economic Life." *Capitalism and Society* 8, no. 2 (2013).

Ricardo, David. *On the Principles of Political Economy and Taxation*. London: John Murray, 1817.

Richtel, Matt. "Can't Take It with You, But You Want More." *New York Times*, January 5, 2014.

Robb, Richard. "Nietzsche and the Economics of Becoming." *Capitalism and Society* 4, no. 1 (2009).

Ross, Don. "Economic Models of Procrastination." In *The Thief of Time: Philosophical Essays on Procrastination*, edited by Chrisoula Andreou and Mark D. White, 28–50. Oxford: Oxford University Press, 2010.

Roth, Alvin E., Vesna Prasnikar, Masahiro Okuno-Fujiwara, and Shmuel Zamir. "Bargaining and Market Behavior in Jerusalem, Ljubljana, Pittsburgh and Tokyo: An Experimental Study." *American Economic Review* 81, no. 5 (1991): 1068–1095.

Russell, Bertrand. *The Problems of Philosophy*. New York: Henry Holt, 1912.

Sartre, Jean-Paul. *Existentialism Is a Humanism*. Edited by John Kulka, translated by Carol Macomber. New Haven: Yale University Press, 2007.

Schopenhauer, Arthur. *On the Fourfold Root of the Principle of Sufficient Reason*. Translated by Eric F. J. Payne. La Salle, IL: Open Court, 1974.

———. *The World as Will and Idea*. 7th ed. Vols. 1–3. Translated by Richard B. Haldane and John Kemp. London: Kegan Paul, Trench, Trübner & Co., 1909.

Schwartz, Barry. *The Paradox of Choice: Why More Is Less*. New York: Harper Collins, 2004.

Searle, John. "Philosophy of Society, Lecture 20." UC Berkeley Philosophy Department, Fall 2010. https://www.youtube.com/watch?v=8Yv1pFIxwT4 (accessed February 2, 2019).

Seligman, Martin E. P. *Flourish: A Visionary New Understanding of Happiness and Well-Being*. New York: Free Press, 2011.

Sen, Amartya. "Maximization and the Act of Choice." *Econometrica* 65, no. 4 (1997): 745–779.

Shakespeare, William. *Macbeth*. New York: Simon and Schuster, 2003.

Sharot, Tali, Cristina M. Velasquez, and Raymond J. Dolan. "Do Decisions Shape Preference? Evidence from Blind Choice." *Psychological Science* 21, no. 9 (2010): 1231–1235.

Simon, Herbert A. "Rational Choice and the Structure of the Environment." *Psychological Review* 63, no. 2 (1956): 129–138.

Singer, Peter. "The Drowning Child and the Expanding Circle." *New Internationalist*, April 5, 1997. https://newint.org/features/1997/04/05/peter -singer-drowning-child-new-internationalist (accessed February 2, 2019).

Bibliography

Skidelsky, Robert. *John Maynard Keynes: The Economist as Saviour, 1920–1937.* London: Macmillan, 1992.

Smith, Adam. *An Inquiry into the Nature and Causes of the Wealth of Nations.* Chicago: University of Chicago Press, 1976.

———. *The Theory of Moral Sentiments.* London: A. Millar, 1759.

Sturges, Preston. *The Palm Beach Story.* Motion picture. Paramount Pictures, 1942.

Taylor, Michael. *Rationality and the Ideology of Disconnection.* Cambridge, UK: Cambridge University Press, 2006.

Thaler, Richard H. "Toward a Positive Theory of Consumer Choice." *Journal of Economic Behavior and Organization* 1 (1980): 39–60.

Thomson, Judith Jarvis. "The Trolley Problem." *Yale Law Journal* 94, no. 6 (1985): 1395–1415.

Tversky, Amos, and Eldar Shafir. "The Disjunction Effect in Choice under Uncertainty." *Psychological Science* 3, no. 5 (1992): 305–309.

Twain, Mark. *Tom Sawyer Abroad, Tom Sawyer, Detective, and Other Stories.* New York: Harper & Brothers, 1896.

Veblen, Thorstein. "The Limitations of Marginal Utility." *Journal of Political Economy* 17, no. 9 (1909): 620–636.

Viner, Jacob. "The Utility Concept in Value Theory and Its Critics: The Utility Concept in Welfare Economics." *Journal of Political Economy* 33, no. 6 (1925): 638–659.

de Waal, Frans B. M., Kristin Leimgruber, and Amanda R. Greenberg. "Giving Is Self-Rewarding for Monkeys." *Proceedings of the National Academy of Sciences* 105, no. 36 (2008): 13685–13689.

Wang, Long, Deepak Malhotra, and J. Keith Murnighan. "Economics Education and Greed." *Academy of Management Learning & Education* 10, no. 4 (2011): 643–660.

Whitman, Walt. 1855. "Song of Myself." In *The Walt Whitman Archive,* edited by Ed Folsom and Kenneth M. Price. whitmanarchive.org (accessed February 2, 2019).

Williams, Bernard. "Persons, Character and Morality." In Williams, *Moral Luck,* 1–19. Cambridge, UK: Cambridge University Press, 1981.

Zarnowski, Frank. *American Work-Sports: A History of Competitions for Cornhuskers, Lumberjacks, Firemen and Others.* Jefferson, NC: McFarland & Co., 2013.

Zeckhauser, Richard J. "Investing in the Unknown and Unknowable." *Capitalism and Society* 1, no. 2 (2006).

Acknowledgments

My most profound thanks go to my editor, Seth Ditchik. Seth conceived of the book nine years ago and nudged me back on track the many times I veered off. He distilled the message into one clear sentence the first time we met: "Besides rational choice and behavioral economics, there's a third thing—acting on the world—and I think that's a book."

The rest of the wonderful team at Yale worked so hard and cared so much. Karen Olson and Ann-Marie Imbornoni gracefully shepherded a Word document into a book. And when they told me "Julie Carlson is a terrific copyeditor," they weren't kidding. Julie—thank you for the vigilance applied to every page.

Over the years, I have accumulated a debt to many others. I am grateful to Edmund Phelps for showing me that neoclassical economics is not the whole story and to James Heckman for

Acknowledgments

pushing me to treat neoclassical economics with the respect it deserves. With the exception of Professors Heckman and Phelps, no one taught me more than my son, Nathan. Thanks to the students in my seminar, Foundations of Individual Choice, at Columbia's School of International and Public Affairs in the fall semesters of 2012, 2014, 2015, 2016, and 2017, who let me test my material. I would like to thank David Nirenberg (who provided encouragement twice when I needed it), Stephen Kosslyn, Robert Kiernan, Matthew Wittman, Mike Woodford, Caitlin Cooper (for positive feedback, not only corrections), Jeff Friedman (who showed me how to think more clearly about the limits of what we can know), Roman Frydman, Cora Weissbourd, Valeria Zhavoronkina, and especially an anonymous referee. Sarika Bansal graciously read the book when it was raw and provided me with many corrections, both literary and conceptual.

In the winter of 2015–2016, I worked side by side on Grove Street mornings and weekends with my daughter, Alice—Alice on the proposal for her book on the science of dreams and me on *Willful: How We Choose What We Do.* During that happy, productive time I ran lots of ideas by her, so I thank her for all the input.

I would have been lost without the dedicated editing of Caitlin Campbell. Not only do I value her fact-checking (for example, "Tolstoy didn't mean what you think he meant, so you have to cut that bit or find a new example"), but I also found her relentless idea-checking amazing. Caitlin is smart, careful, and patient beyond measure. I'm so lucky I found her.

232

My funny, loyal, brilliant friend Susan Lee showed me how clear writing could lead to clear thinking, that nothing would be lost by cutting highfalutin words, and how to construct a book that someone outside of my inner circle of friends might be willing to read. I will acknowledge once and for all: when we argued, Susan was (almost) always right. I would also like to thank her husband, Ken Weisshaar, for being a sounding board for Susan while she was helping me and for feeding her ice cream to keep her going.

Without Reihan Salam, this book would never have been written. Reihan read my article "Nietzsche and the Economics of Becoming," wrote about it, and brought it to Seth's attention. Thanks, too, to the publishers who permitted me to quote their songs: *Can't Buy Me Love*, words and music by John Lennon and Paul McCartney, copyright © 1964 Sony/ATV Music Publishing LLC, copyright renewed, all rights administered by Sony/ATV Music Publishing LLC, 424 Church Street, Suite 1200, Nashville, TN, 37219, international copyright secured, all rights reserved, reprinted by permission of Hal Leonard LLC; *Busted*, words and music by Harlan Howard, copyright © 1962 Sony/ATV Music Publishing LLC, copyright renewed, all rights administered by Sony/ATV Music Publishing LLC, 424 Church Street, Suite 1200, Nashville, TN, 37219, international copyright secured, all rights reserved, reprinted by permission of Hal Leonard LLC; *Another Brick in the Wall*, words and music by Roger Waters, copyright © 1979 Roger Waters Music Overseas, Ltd.,

My wife, Ianthe Jeanne Dugan, to whom this book is dedicated, has helped me over many years with both ideas and words. She somehow managed to encourage me while delivering the message: it's still not good enough. I would jump in the river to save her any day.

Index

Index

Index

Philip II, king of Macedonia, 181
planning, 149–151; for consumption, 154–157; long-term vs.
short-term, 148–149; rational
choice applied to, 152–158, 162
play, 44–45, 167, 202
pleasure-pain principle, 18
Plutarch, 180–181
Poe, Edgar Allan, 126
pollution, 132–133
Popeye the Sailor Man, 19
portfolio theory, 64–65
positive psychology (happiness
research), 25–26, 201–202
preferences, 18–19, 198; aggregating, 38–39, 132, 164; altruism
and, 28, 38, 45, 104, 110, 111,
116; in behavioral economics, 24,
168; beliefs' feedback into, 51, 55;
defined, 23; intransitive, 158–159;
in purposeful behavior, 25, 36;
risk aversion and, 51; stability
of, 33, 115, 147, 207, 208; "time-
inconsistent," 158, 159, 166, 203
present value, 7, 139
principal-agent problem, 72
Principles of Economics (Marshall), 41
prisoner's dilemma, 105
private equity, 75
procrastination, 3, 4, 19, 177–178
prospect theory, 168
protectionism, 185–187
Prussia, 191
public equities, 75
punishment, 109
purposeful choice, 22–26, 27, 34, 36,
56, 133–134, 204–205; altruism
compatible with, 104, 113–114,

115–116; commensurability and,
153–154; as default rule, 43–46;
expert opinion and, 57; extreme
unexpected events and, 62–63;
flow of time and, 30; for-itself
behavior commingled with,
40–43, 129, 171; mechanistic
quality of, 68; in merchant's
choice, 135, 137–138; Pareto
efficiency linked to, 132; rational
choice distinguished from, 22–23;
regret linked to, 128; social relations linked to, 28; stable preferences linked to, 33; in trolley
problem, 135–136; vaccination
and, 58–59; wage increases and,
187. *See also* rational choice

quests, 30–31

Rapaczynski, Andrzej, 220n24
Raskob, John Jakob, 211–212n12
rational choice: behavioral economics reconciled with, 6, 10; changes
of mind consistent with, 147,
149–151; comparison inherent
in, 37–39, 196; defined, 22–23;
individual preferences accommodated by, 198; insights of, 5, 10,
21, 24–25, 138–139; perils and
shortcomings of, 7–8, 12, 14, 21,
52, 55; purposeful choice distinguished from, 22–23; social
relations unexplained by, 12;
stable preferences linked to, 115.
See also purposeful choice
rationalization, 15, 43–44, 55,
159–162, 178, 194–195